Portfolio Models: Reflections Across the Teaching Profession

Portfolio Models: Reflections Across the Teaching Profession

Maureen McLaughlin
East Stroudsburg University

Mary Ellen Vogt
California State University Long Beach

Joanne A. Anderson,
Judy DuMez,
Marian Graeven Peter
Cardinal Stritch College

Alyce Hunter
West Windsor Plainsboro Middle School

Credits

Every effort has been made to contact copyright holders for permission to reproduce borrowed material where necessary. We apologize for any oversights and would be happy to rectify them in future printings.

Christopher-Gordon Publishers, Inc.
1502 Providence Highway, Suite #12
Norwood, MA 02062
Tel: (800) 934-8322

Printed in the United States of America

10 9 8 7 6 5 4 3 2 1   03 02 01 00 99 98

ISBN: 0-926842-74-9

Short Contents

Contents

Section II
Portfolio Presentations in Teacher Education: Rites of Passage for the Emerging Professional 77

Joanne Anderson, Judith Du Mez, and *Marian Graeven Peter*

Forms and Figures

Preface

Designing meaningful assessment systems that are congruent with contemporary theoretical beliefs is a constant challenge for educators. The focus of many of these efforts is classroom assessment, however, not teacher evaluation procedures. The current use of performance and portfolio assessments with students makes the incongruity between innovative student assessment practices and the more traditional methods through which educators themselves are assessed even more acute. As a result, administrators and supervisors have been searching for an authentic way to evaluate teaching performance, while teachers have been seeking more diverse ways to document their teaching effectiveness. *Portfolio Models: Reflections Across the Teaching Profession* was written in response to these needs. The book is designed to inform preservice and inservice teachers, school and university administrators, teacher educators, and professional development specialists about portfolio models in various educational contexts that will facilitate teacher assessment, evaluation, and change.

Portfolio Models: Reflections Across the Teaching Profession features three professionally situated applications of portfolio assessment. Each is clearly delineated and presented in practical format. Examples from those who have used the models illustrate how each functions within a particular setting. The book is divided into three sections: *Portfolio Assessment for Inservice Teachers: A Collaborative Model* opens the volume, followed by *Portfolio Presentations in Teacher Education: Rites of Passage for the Emerging Professional,* and *The Power, Production, and Promise of Portfolios for Novice and Seasoned Teachers* concludes the volume.

Section I, *Portfolio Assessment for Inservice Teachers: A Collaborative Model*, focuses on the alignment of innovative assessment practices with inservice teacher evaluation. This five-part section begins with a detailed theoretical framework for using performance portfolios for teacher evaluation. It then describes the Collaborative Model and its five categories: Educational Philosophy, Professional Development, Curriculum and Instruction, Student Growth, and Contributions to School and Community. This is followed by an explanation of the collegial nature of the Model and a description of how the portfolio process functions. It also includes excerpts from performances developed by elementary, middle, and high school teachers, as well as extensive lists of teacher-generated goals for each category of the Model. Teacher and administrator reactions to the Model and implications for the portfolio are also featured. Sample forms used to monitor the portfolio process, the standards for evaluating the portfolios, and a question and answer section conclude Section I.

Section II, *Portfolio Presentations in Teacher Education: Rites of Passage for the Emerging Professional*, discusses portfolio assessment as an effective and authentic means of measuring growth and achievement in preservice teacher education. In this context, the portfolio is viewed as a criterion for admission to the professional level of course work; admission to student teaching; and cataloging and showcasing acquired skills, attitudes, and beliefs for job interviews. In this model, the portfolio, together with additional criteria connecting all aspects of teacher education, serves as the critical demonstration of developing and acquired teacher competence. The format for developing a portfolio process, complete with forms, rubrics, and organization and orientation guidelines, is thoroughly delineated.

Secion III, *The Power, Production, and Promise of Portfolios for Novice and Seasoned Teachers*, describes developing teacher portfolios, extending the concept to include administrators. Portfolios are presented as guides for reflection and empowerment: They promote methods of enhancing professional growth for all teachers and administrators, whether they are exemplary, below average, or somewhere in between. The presentation of the portfolio to administration and peers as well as the value of the portfolio to the producer are discussed. It is emphasized that the production of the portfolio is not a goal in itself, but rather is a means to attaining higher objectives such as teacher and administrator self-renewal, improved student learning, and school reform. Examples from the experiences of teachers who have developed portfolios are featured.

While each model has distinctive qualities, the following beliefs are common to all:

- Portfolios offer a meaningful way to assess and evaluate educators' performance.
- Creating and maintaining portfolios in any educational context is time-consuming, but the rewards far outweigh the demands.

- Portfolios provide a focus for those creating them as well as for those evaluating them.
- Reflection is a highly valued component of portfolio development.
- Assessment and evaluation are dynamic, ongoing processes.

The benefits of using these portfolio assessment models are numerous: They enable participants to align current educational theory with innovative practice, they offer individuals an opportunity to witness personal growth over time, they afford participants an active role in the assessment and evaluation processes, they empower those who use them, and they facilitate change. Further, those who create and maintain portfolios based on these models engage in unique learning experiences. None of the models asks participants to demonstrate minimum abilities. Rather, each model encourages individuals to attain their personal best—to demonstrate their maximum potentials.

The educators with whom we have interacted in developing these models have been an inspiration to us. Many have acknowledged that these innovative assessment systems have created positive change in their contexts. We share the models with you, hoping they will impact not only your personal role in education, but your vision of assessment and evaluation as well.

Portfolio Assessment for Inservice Teachers: A Collaborative Model

Section I

Section I

Portfolio Assessment for Inservice Teachers: A Collaborative Model

Maureen McLaughlin
MaryEllen Vogt

Much as in other professions, performance has been the foundation for inservice teacher evaluation for many years. It has, however, been embedded in a process that is one-dimensional: An administrator observing a teacher and making judgments about performance (Glickman & Bey, 1990; Goldhammer, Anderson, & Krajewski, 1980). Regarding this practice, Shulman (1988, p. 39) has observed, "Too often the typical observation method for evaluating teaching is like photographing the Mona Lisa with a black and white Polaroid camera or like tape-recording the most sumptuous Carmen with an office Dictaphone. So much potential, so limited a harvest."

In the teaching profession today, both traditional and innovative methods of teacher evaluation are being used. Consider the following scenarios.

Scenario One

Sharon Hollingsworth assesses her second-grade students' math, reading, and writing progress through performance portfolios. In contrast, Sharon's own performance as a teacher is observed and evaluated through a structured and widely used method called clinical supervision (Goldhammer, Anderson, & Krajewski, 1980).

Sharon has been teaching second grade for eight years. At the end of her third year, she was granted tenure based upon satisfactory performance during the probationary period, her first three years of teaching. While on probation, Sharon's principal scheduled several formal observations, each of which included pre- and post-

---

conferences. The principal's observations focused primarily on aspects of teaching identified during the pre-conferences.

Sharon's current teaching contract requires that she is observed a minimum of once each year, with the principal submitting a written response following the post-observation conference. Sharon has the opportunity to reply to the principal's comments on the evaluation form. In essence, the principal's written evaluation of the observation constitutes the primary evidence of Sharon's overall effectiveness as a teacher.

Scenario Two

In a neighboring school district, Juan Gallegos is beginning his seventh year of teaching fifth grade. He, too, has developed an effective process for implementing performance portfolios in his classroom. Like Sharon, Juan was tenured after completing a successful three-year probationary period. However, his annual evaluation includes a process that is very different from Sharon's. Juan's district uses the Collaborative Model of Teacher Evaluation.

At the beginning of each year, in collaboration with his principal and a group of co-teachers, Juan establishes specific teaching goals related to five broad areas of education (philosophy of education, curriculum and instruction, professional development, student growth, and contributions to school and community). These goals may be continued from the previous year, but will also include new goals written specifically for the current group of children he is teaching. Throughout the school year, Juan gathers evidences of his progress in meeting these goals. His principal is a member of a team of teachers and administrators that helped Juan establish his goals. Because of this, the principal is able to support and assist Juan through scheduled observations, conferencing, opportunities for professional development, and collaborative activities designed to champion the school's mission and further each teacher's goals. Juan's performance as a teacher is evaluated in an ongoing, collaborative, multifaceted, multidimensional, and highly reflective manner.

It is clear that these two teachers are involved in decidedly different evaluation processes. While the first is considered acceptable practice in many school districts, the second represents an innovative model of evaluation based upon current assessment research (Hiebert, Valencia, & Afflerbach, 1994; McLaughlin & Kennedy, 1993). Within this model, it is possible to include not only scheduled observations and conferences, but also many other types of evidences that capture the dynamic nature of teaching and learning.

Using portfolios for teacher evaluation, however, has been limited. Perhaps this is because a reputable model that would encourage school districts to consider portfolio assessment as a viable method of teacher evaluation has not been available.

The Collaborative Model of Teacher Evaluation (see Figure I-1) was created in response to this void (McLaughlin & Vogt, 1995). The Model is practical and multifaceted and is endorsed by both teachers and administrators. In addition, the portfolio process embedded in the Model is goal-based and designed to document teacher performance over time.

The Collaborative Model is fully described in this section of the book. Part One of the section begins by offering a review of the theoretical underpinnings that support the Model's development. Topics include the changing role of the teacher, theories of teaching and learning, an historical view of assessment, and assessment innovations.

Part Two offers an overview of the Collaborative Model and describes each of the Model's categories: Educational Philosophy, Professional Development, Curriculum and Instruction, Student Growth, and Contributions to School and Community. Part Two also presents a step-by-step guide for using the Model effectively, explains the portfolio process, and illustrates how the Model functions in diverse contexts.

Part Three features reactions to the Collaborative Model. Comments of both teachers and administrators focus on the Model's strengths as well as areas of concern.

Part Four presents examples of teacher-generated goals and evidences for each category of the Model. The diversity of gcal statements and performances featured in Part Four demonstrates individual teacher's ownership of the process.

The Conclusion addresses implications for the portfolio culture and speculates on the role of the Collaborative Model in the history of teacher evaluation.

Five appendixes included at the end of this section contain information designed to facilitate implementation and management of the Collaborative Model. Appendixes A, B, C, and D feature the Portfolio Planner, standards of evaluation, and team member rubrics. Appendix E presents a Question and Answer framework in which collective bargaining agreements, professional development, time factors, weighting goals, teacher performance, the role of observation, and reliability and validity issues are discussed.

PART ONE: THEORETICAL UNDERPINNINGS

A CHANGING DEFINITION OF THE TEACHER

School reform and the improvement of teaching have been issues of discussion for decades. Over the years, educators have attempted to improve teaching by systematically and periodically evaluating teachers' performance in the classroom. Ostensibly, the purpose for these periodic evaluations was to improve teaching in order to better student learning outcomes. However, John Dewey pointed to the need for systemic change in education when he stated in 1904, "The thing needful is improvement to education, not simply by turning out teachers who can do better the things that are necessary to do, but rather by changing the conception of what constitutes education" (p. 30).

Several contemporary documents have also called for systemic change in education. In 1983, the National Commission on Excellence in Education's publication, *A Nation at Risk: The Imperative for Educational Reform,* emerged as the most dramatic critique of teaching and teacher preparation. Responding to *A Nation at Risk,* the Carnegie Forum on Education and the Economy (1986) and the Holmes Group (1986, 1990) focused on self-improvement in teachers and teaching, and more meaningful, relevant experiences for teachers-in-training.

It is hard to change beliefs about what constitutes "education." Some researchers have suggested that reform efforts may be more likely to succeed when educational stakeholders such as teachers, administrators, and teacher educators collaborate. Others, including Dewey (1933), suggested that inquiry and reflection about pedagogy are critical to effecting change. Inherent in Dewey's thinking was that there should be no dichotomy between theory and practice. Rather, he suggested that teachers refine their practice by developing new theories based upon their own direct experiences. These practical experiences are then applied to the theories that are further refined, and the cycle continues.

It is interesting that Dewey's beliefs about the role of the teacher are so compatible with current educational reform efforts. Outdated views of the teacher as purveyor of knowledge, as an all-knowing transmitter of information, have yielded to a contemporary vision of the teacher as a reflective facilitator, one who engages students in problem-solving, investigation, and exploration of important issues and concepts.

Today's teachers are encouraged to develop a sense of the "teacher self," a voice refined often in collaboration with other teachers (Acker, 1995). Researchers are increasingly interested in the stories that teachers tell. Hollingsworth (1992) suggested that the idea of collaborative conversation about learning is grounded in feminist principles which honor experience as an important source of knowledge. For today's educators, pedagogical reflection extends beyond self-assessment to the role of the teacher as a coach, helping children to reflect on their own progress, especially within collaborative and cooperative classroom environments (Colton, Sparks-Langer, Tripp-Opple, & Simmons, 1989).

As the role of the teacher changes, as pundits continue to call for educational reform, and as teacher educators strive to prepare new teachers for the challenging responsibilities they will face, it becomes clear that goal-setting, reflection, self-assessment, and collaboration are integral to a teacher's growth and critical for effective teaching (McLaughlin & Vogt, 1996). Current theories of teaching and learning, detailed in the next section, underscore the importance of incorporating these elements in meaningful teacher evaluation practices.

THEORIES OF TEACHING AND LEARNING

Educational theory is the foundation upon which educators develop curriculum, methods, materials, and approaches to assessment, teaching, and learning. Theories are characterized by cohesion, how things fit together. They are developed according to organizing principles or generalizations that explain events, and they hold up under scrutiny and judgment. By necessity, educational theories are flexible; they change and are recast based on evaluation, reevaluation, and incremental evidence (Ruddell, 1996). As with other areas of teaching, current approaches to assessment are based upon a set of integrated and interrelated theories. These include social negotiation, scaffolding, constructivism, collegiality, mentoring, peer coaching, and reflective practice.

Vygotskian Perspectives

The work of Vygotsky has greatly influenced our understanding of how people learn (Vygotsky, 1978; Wink, 1997). Central to Vygotsky's ideas about the relationships among language, cognition, and social interaction is the notion of internalization (Forman & Cazden, 1994). That is, a learner is better able to internalize new concepts and ideas while using language, an "inner speech." During interactions with others, learners develop understandings and generate knowledge within a social context. Collaborative problem-solving in which partners or group members engage in a mutual task, enables participants to complete a task that few or none could have finished alone. This concept of scaffolding, frequently associated with Vygotsky's Zone of Proximal Development, is based on the idea that at the beginning of instruction, learners need a great deal of assistance and support (Cambourne & Turnbill, 1988). Gradually, as less support is needed, it is removed until independence is achieved (Pearson, 1985). If learners are unable to maintain independence, the support system is reinstated until they are able to reach independence once again.

 While initially conceptualized around children's learning, these ideas are also directly related to teacher development. Teachers are life-long learners by necessity and by choice. Their learning and development can be augmented by regular opportunities to interact and collaborate with peers and supervisors who are involved in and supportive of their learning about teaching.

Constructivism

Learners make sense of their world through the connections they make with past experiences, prior knowledge, and current learning (Anderson & Pearson, 1984). They construct meaning through these experiences when they confront relevant problems, engage in inquiry, and are involved in learning activities that build upon previous experience and knowledge. New understandings are developed when these connections are made.

 In the classroom, the teacher's responsibility is to assist students in activating and utilizing their knowledge base and experience in order to make connections to what is being learned. Classroom activities that support and extend students' background knowledge and experience enable children to construct personal meanings and understandings.

 Constructing meaning by connecting prior experience with new learning is relevant for all learners, including teachers. Using current practices to evaluate the relevance of new approaches promotes reflective evaluation. New understandings are developed or constructed when this introspection occurs.

Collegiality, Mentoring, Peer Coaching

As innovative educational practices have evolved, the collegial nature of teaching has offered an ideal context for collaborative inquiry and learning. The paradigm has shifted from teachers closing their doors and teaching, to colleagues openly seeking support and developing trust. This has led to discussions about contemporary instructional methods and reflective conversations about best practice. Numerous benefits have emerged. As Raney and Robbins (1989, p. 38) have noted, "Talking about teaching—reflecting on why they do what they do—has helped teachers develop a genuine appreciation and acceptance of others. Feelings of isolation and passivity have given way to an environment of collaboration and professional growth." Further, Darling-Hammond (1996, p. 9) has observed, "Those who have access to teacher networks, enriched professional roles, and collegial work feel more efficacious in gaining the knowledge they need to meet the needs of their students and more positive about staying in the profession." In addition, Sweeney (1994, p. 229) has noted, "Collegial partnership offers teachers an opportunity to form and develop strong relationships to improve teaching." Such collegiality is the foundation of both the mentoring and peer coaching processes.

In *The Odyssey,* Odysseus gave the responsibility of nurturing his son, Telemachus, to his loyal friend, Mentor. While Odysseus was off fighting the Trojan War, Mentor served as Telemachus's teacher and guide. His modeling set a standard for behavior, and from this example, the term "mentoring" has come to mean an "intentional nurturing, insightful, supportive process" (Odell, 1990, p. 5). Sweeney (1994, p. 234) has further delineated the concept of mentoring: "Mentors have the ability to put theory into practice and the sensitivity and skill to know when and how to help."

While the role of mentoring is well acknowledged in novice-veteran teacher relationships, the concept works equally well for experienced educators who want to learn about a new topic or employ innovative instructional techniques successfully practiced by others. Hardcastle (1988) found that while individuals do search out people to serve as their mentors, more often mentors and protégés find each other in unplanned ways. The collegial nature of the Collaborative Model, affords both teachers and administrators opportunities to establish mentoring relationships.

The concept of peer coaching emerged from a need for teachers to implement and practice concepts presented in staff development seminars. The results were positive: Staff development directly impacted student learning. In the peer coaching process, "teachers learn from one another while planning instruction, developing support materials, watching one another work with students, and thinking together about the impact of their behavior on their students' learning" (Showers & Joyce, 1996, p.15).

Administrative support, training in coaching skills, trust among participants, and program adjustments responsive to the changing needs of staff members are all necessary for successful peer coaching (Chase & Wolf, 1989). While the greatest benefit of this concept is often considered to be higher quality instruction, other positive outcomes have been reported:

"The sense of individual and group pride that develops from this appraisal process is overwhelming. Teachers no longer take for granted what they and their peers accomplish each day in the classroom. They realize the strength that lies in diversity. Through networking, teachers discover they are their own best resources. This is the key that makes the process succeed" (Whalen & DeRose, 1993, p.48).

"Our peer assistance program has made us aware of a different kind of professional accountability—not the accountability measured in a formal evaluation by an administrator, but the kind that recognizes our responsibility for helping each other grow and improve. We can help each other challenge our own limits, and we can challenge the isolation that imposes artificial limits" (Chrisco, 1989, p.32).

Collegiality is a critical characteristic of the changing concept of the teacher. It invites reflection and professional growth (Whalen & DeRose, 1993) and promotes teachers' understandings of its role in the students' learning processes.

Reflective Practitioner

Self-reflection is a key factor in portfolio assessment. It requires the participants to think about what they are doing, why they are doing it, what the outcomes are, and how the information can be used for continuous improvement. Simultaneously, it engenders ownership of the assessment process and shows that the thoughts of those being assessed are valued. Self-reflection also provides access to information about thinking processes which is not sought in more traditional types of assessment (McLaughlin & Vogt, 1996).

When using the Collaborative Model, reflection occurs at multiple stages during the assessment process. Reflection is evident as the teacher creates goals within each category, analyzes various evidences, creates reflective statements, participates in portfolio conversations, and develops a self-evaluation of the portfolio. The integration of reflection throughout the process offers opportunities for those creating portfolios to experience reflection-on-action, reflection-in-action, and reflection-for-action (Schon, 1987; Killion & Todnem, 1991). Reagan, Case, Case, & Freiberg (1993) noted that while these three types of reflection are generally associated with the teaching process, reflection is not linear; it is better viewed as a spiral activity in which the result of one type of reflection leads to another. Because it is such a prevalent and valued component of the Collaborative Model, reflection is an important focus of the professional development plan.

The role of reflection in portfolio assessment complements the idea of the teacher as a reflective practitioner. As educators engage in instruction, they reflect on what they are teaching and how effective the lesson is. Such reflections offer insights into various dimensions of the teaching and learning process that can lead to better teaching (Schon, 1987). In the Collaborative Model, reflection leads to improved instruction and offers direction for the creation of future goals.

As teachers engage in reflection, they become better thinkers and, consequently, better practitioners. "Teachers develop problem-solving skills in examining their experiences, generating their alternatives, and evaluating their actions. These skills allow them to model risk-taking, open-mindedness, and continuous learning for their students" (Blake et al., 1995, p.39).

HISTORICAL VIEW OF ASSESSMENT

One constant in education is that it is ever-changing. Keeping current with educational innovation is a challenge for educators at all levels. New theories, methods, and materials are proposed, researched, and implemented; seemingly as these are put into practice, a new wave of contemporary theories and approaches is recommended, and the cycle begins anew.

During the past two decades, in keeping with calls for educational reform, assessment practices have changed dramatically. Traditionally, educational evaluation within the classroom involved administering quizzes, or tests. These evaluations were supplemented with standardized tests used for diverse purposes such as student placement, district accountability, and determining federal funding of educational programs (McLaughlin & Vogt, 1996).

However, it has become increasingly clear that traditional standardized testing is insufficient as a measure of student progress because it offers little information about how students engage in the learning process. While their results are used to define student achievement, standardized tests exclude any measure of student development. Most standardized tests are not coordinated with district standards for learning, and test results are therefore questionable. They do not permit students to engage in using varied learning strategies, are poor predictors of individual performance, and are used to classify and label students (McLaughlin, 1995; Winograd, Paris, & Bridge, 1991; Worthen, 1993).

During the late 1970s and early 1980s, large-scale minimum competency testing was implemented throughout the country in an attempt to boost student performance. However, numerous problems with minimum competency testing were uncovered: (a) Only one test was used to measure a student's performance, (b) The measures were structured similarly to standardized tests, (c) Issues of validity arose, (d) The testing represented a restricted view of the educational process, and (e) The testing focused on each child's minimum performance level rather than his or her maximum potential (McLaughlin, 1995). Because of the problems inherent with both standardized and minimum competency testing, Pikulski (1990) and others urged educators to focus assessment and evaluation efforts on decreasing the misuses of standardized testing, improving existing tests, and developing new, innovative means of assessing student progress and performance.

Although classroom assessment practices have evolved in recent years, the traditional method of observation by an administrator to evaluate a teacher has remained virtually unchanged. Such observations have occurred annually or on a few occasions throughout the academic year. In this process, the administrator has traditionally been viewed as the supervisor or inspector, and the teacher has been the person being inspected (Airasian, 1993).

A review of the literature indicates that observation alone is ineffective and rarely results in improved teacher performance or professional growth (Blake et al., 1995; Dagley & Orso, 1991; Haefele, 1993; Regan, 1993; Setteducati, 1995; Sweeney, 1994; Wood, 1992). Specifically, Olivero and Heck's (1994) review of research concerning teacher observation revealed that it has failed to:

- Nurture competent teachers.
- Help beginning teachers make the transition from novice to experienced.
- Challenge accomplished educators.
- Assess and improve school leadership skills.
- Engender ownership of the evaluation process.
- Distinguish between teachers at different career levels.
- Provide a process to eliminate those who have not emerged as quality teachers.

The information presented by these researchers, accompanied by a growing awareness of the changing role of the teacher and a need for more innovative classroom assessment practices, caused the educational community to develop more meaningful assessment methods.

ASSESSMENT INNOVATIONS

The innovative view of assessment that emerged focuses on authenticity and performance (Paris, 1991; Shepard, 1989; Tierney, Carter, & Desai, 1991; Valencia, 1990). Assessments based on authenticity and performance address not only the learner's knowledge, but also the practical application of knowledge through meaningful tasks.

Portfolio assessment may be the perfect method for organizing these innovative assessments to describe student progress over time. It includes goal-setting on the part of both teacher and student, gathering authentic evidences, reflecting, and conferencing. Because the student has ownership of the process and engages in reflection, the teacher truly has the opportunity to understand each pupil's learning process (McLaughlin, 1995). Furthermore, because it employs multiple indicators, portfolio assessment accommodates students' personal learning styles (Vogt, McLaughlin, & Ruddell, 1993).

As portfolio assessment of students has become increasingly prevalent in school districts (Hiebert, Valencia, & Afflerbach, 1994), it also has become more widely used in preservice teacher education programs (Barton & Collins, 1993). Implementing portfolio assessment in the evaluation of inservice teachers appears to be the next logical step in systemic change (ASCD, 1995; Kieffer, 1994; Lomask, Pecheone, & Boykoff-Baron, 1995; McLaughlin & Vogt, 1995).

TEACHER EVALUATION TODAY: A CALL FOR CONGRUENCE

"The crisis of education is not that schools are no longer what they once were; the crisis is that schools are precisely what they once were while the world around them is undergoing profound revolution" (Barth, 1993, p.219). The idea expressed in this statement applies to the stagnant nature of traditional teacher evaluation policies. Although the educational process has undergone myriad changes, the process of evaluating teachers has not evolved. While portfolio assessment has been embraced for school and university students, the teacher evaluation process has, remarkably, remained virtually unchanged.

Although many teachers are still being evaluated through observation alone, they find themselves using portfolio assessment and other innovative practices to evaluate their students. Teachers know that portfolio assessment is dynamic, authentic, reliable and multifaceted. They understand that it accommodates individual learning styles as well as cultural and linguistic differences. They realize that it encourages the use of personal strengths to demonstrate progress, but also documents needs. Evaluation through observation alone does not share these attributes. The incongruency is clear.

A call for the creation of more meaningful teacher evaluation processes has emerged. Poole (1995, p. 565) labeled it a "transition from hierarchical to collegial relationships between teachers and administrators." Black (1993, p. 38) saw schools rethinking the teacher evaluation process because "many schools deep into restructuring are designing evaluation systems to fit with new theories of classroom teaching and learning." Levine (1993, p. 223) described the school as "a workplace that pays too little attention to supporting and promoting adult development." Blake et al. (1995, p. 37) noted that "teachers should not be viewed as needing supervision and inspection, but as professionals who can provide their own self-assessment, teaching improvement, and professional growth."

Haefele (1993) suggested that formative and summative purposes should serve as the foundation of meaningful teacher evaluation systems. Formative assessment is an ongoing process concerned with the development and improvement of teacher performance. Summative pertains to making decisions for accountability purposes, such as promoting or terminating (Dagley & Orso, 1991; Haefele, 1993).

Barth (1993) described personal goal-setting and interaction with adults as two essential components of the teacher evaluation process. The interaction focuses primarily on the power of modeling and is personified through such processes as peer coaching, peer observation, mentoring, and study groups.

Portfolio assessment encompasses all of these elements. Regan (1993, p. 289) summarized the advantages of using portfolios for teacher evaluation by noting that they:

- Generate information about the cognitive aspects of teaching.
- Explicitly connect teaching to student outcomes.
- Offer differentiated evaluation processes for novice and experienced teachers.
- Stimulate rich, intellectual conversations among teachers and between teachers and administrators.
- Assume accountability as an accepted professional norm.
- Function without inordinate demands on administrator time.
- Lead teachers to internalize standards for excellence in teaching related directly to student learning.
- Shift responsibility for documenting proficiency from the administrator to the teacher.

Embedding innovative assessment practices in teacher evaluation procedures encourages educators' ownership of the process, nurtures professional growth, and fosters self-esteem. The result is teachers who are actively involved in their evaluations and who no longer need to accept one individual's analysis of their teaching ability based on a one-shot observation (Black, 1993).

PART TWO: THE COLLABORATIVE MODEL OF TEACHER EVALUATION

With a redefinition of the teacher's role, development of theories of learning that support personal construction of meaning, changes in teaching methods and materials, and innovations in assessing student performance, it is only logical that the process of evaluating teaching effectiveness should experience similar development. In keeping with current theories of learning, the Collaborative Model offers an innovative means of supporting teachers as they learn and grow in their profession.

As seen in Figure I-1, the Collaborative Model is based upon five broad categories: Educational Philosophy, Professional Development, Curriculum and Instruction, Student Growth, and Contributions to School and Community. These components emerged from discussions with and surveys completed by inservice teachers and administrators. They are designed to offer a general framework for the portfolio process, while simultaneously accommodating each teacher's individuality as well as each school district's needs.

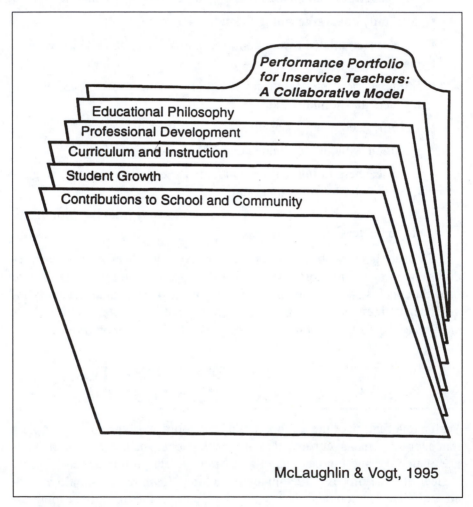

Figure I-1 Collaborative Model

The Collaborative Model is structured to accommodate a multidimensional, collegial vision of teacher evaluation that offers active roles to teachers and administrators. It provides educational stakeholders with a broader perspective concerning the nature and scope of professional practice. The Model offers teachers increased ownership of the assessment process, is congruent with national models of teacher excellence such as the *National Board of Professional Teaching Standards,* and can exist within the confines of collective bargaining agreements. It extends the innovative assessment practices that are commonly used with their students to the teachers themselves.

Finally, the Collaborative Model includes, but does not solely rely on, observation in the teacher evaluation process. Observations may be submitted as partial evidence of teacher performance within any of the categories of the Collaborative Model, but they emerge as only one of several indicators of teacher performance. This model, therefore, offers a dynamic view of the teacher as opposed to the snapshot, limited view offered by observation alone.

Current theories of teaching and learning are embedded in the Collaborative Model. The process begins with the assumption that the teacher is a lifelong learner who constructs new knowledge and understandings through reflective inquiry. The social context of the classroom and the personal teaching and learning experiences of the teacher serve as the foundation for goal-setting and a variety of evidences. The principal or other supervisor is involved in the evaluation process from its inception and serves not only as one of the evaluators, but also as a mentor or guide. Assistance and support are scaffolded throughout the process with multiple opportunities for collaboration with peers and administrators central to the evaluation process. The Collaborative Model virtually ensures reflectivity, an essential catalyst for teacher growth and development. From goal-setting through selection of evidences, self-assessment rationale statements, and portfolio conversations, the teacher reflects on what has worked and what has not, and why.

THE CATEGORIES OF THE COLLABORATIVE MODEL

Educational Philosophy, Professional Development, Curriculum and Instruction, Student Growth, and Contributions to School and Community are the categories within the Collaborative Model of Teacher Evaluation. Descriptions of each category and examples of how the Model functions in representative educational contexts follow.

Educational Philosophy

This category encourages teachers to reflect on basic core beliefs about teaching and learning. Because education typically exists in a state of change, regularly offering new ideas and trends, teachers need to be challenged to examine what motivates the decisions they make. As with other aspects of portfolio development, goal-setting is integral to establishing an educational philosophy.

Although many teacher education programs require preservice teachers to write a philosophical statement about their beliefs, once certified, the teacher's philosophy of education is seldom discussed or thought about. However, as teachers become more experienced, they generally develop new beliefs, refine old ones, and build new theories about teaching and learning. These in turn guide instruction and the selection of materials and methods. Also, most school districts require teachers to continually update their knowledge through course work and professional development. New knowledge acquired through continuing education impacts instruction and, consequently, the teacher's educational philosophy.

Reflecting on one's developing philosophy, articulating it, and sharing it with other educators leads to growth. In the Collaborative Model, teachers establish goals related to the development of their philosophy and then gather evidence of their progress in reaching these goals.

An educator's evolving educational philosophy is exemplified by a science teacher who set a goal to restructure her teaching from a more traditional, teacher-centered model to a more response-centered, student-focused approach. The change in her thinking was gradual as she contemplated what she needed to do to reach this goal. She read journal articles, conversed with and observed the classrooms of teachers she admired, and enlisted the support of a peer coach. As her philosophy about teaching became more apparent, she made changes in her classroom, confident that she was making decisions based upon a well-thought-out belief system, not whim or fad.

Professional Development

Throughout their careers, teachers are expected to participate in professional development experiences that are intended to improve their teaching effectiveness. In some states or school districts, proof of continuing education may be required for salary advancement or recertification. Many teachers also participate in local, state, and national professional organizations that offer regular opportunities for inservice. However, choices about professional growth are often unfocused, and unless the teachers are enrolled in university graduate education programs, there is generally no accountability for what has been learned or applied from professional development experiences. In fact, teachers report that even though they learn many new ideas from courses and workshops, they infrequently implement the ideas into their own teaching.

Within the Collaborative Model, however, teachers establish personal learning goals that help to focus their professional growth opportunities. When teachers choose to study independently, attend courses, or participate in other professional development opportunities that focus on the goal(s) they have created for themselves, professional development becomes more purposeful, reflective, and personally meaningful.

Because goal-setting for professional development is determined in a collaborative manner, the site administrator or supervisor as well as other teachers participate in the creation of the goals. Goals may be institutional, relating to district standards, reform, and/or innovative projects being undertaken in the district or school, or they may be personal, involving areas that need improvement or issues that the teacher wishes to explore.

The following cases illustrate the Collaborative Model's professional development category: One primary teacher chose to increase his knowledge of constructivism, one of his personal learning goals, by attending appropriate sessions at a national conference. Another decided to increase her awareness of multiple intelligences by participating in a local series of seminars. After attending the seminars, the teacher created a study group with opportunities for peer coaching and collaboration.

Curriculum and Instruction

This category of the Collaborative Model promotes growth in curriculum development and instruction by encouraging teachers to take an active role in curriculum reform not only to learn, but also to implement new methods of instruction. Within this category, teachers assess their contexts, create personal goals to enhance curriculum and instruction, and use the results for continuous improvement.

Goals may be tied to district or state curriculum frameworks or they may be individualized. Sometimes goals for this category will be linked to those established for professional development. For example, if a teacher decides to change some aspect of curriculum and/or instruction, he or she will most likely concentrate on professional development in the respective area, and then will work to implement changes based upon what was learned from the training. The teacher's porfolio will include artifacts that provide evidence of his or her new methods, materials, curriculum, and approaches as well as reflections on the impact of the classroom changes that occurred as a result of the goal-setting.

As examples of growth in the Curriculum and Instruction Category, one middle school language arts teacher submitted examples of his students' writing portfolios to demonstrate his implementation of portfolio assessment. An elementary teacher taught her students how to use e-mail to communicate with students in other parts of the world. Her portfolio included e-mail messages that she and her students had written to and received from a teacher and group of children in Alaska.

Student Growth

This category encourages ongoing reflection about the cause and effect relationship between teaching effectiveness and student progress. Typically, measures of student progress are used to evaluate how well a particular student has performed given tasks. The emphasis on the student's academic performance sheds little light on the teacher's role in helping the student to learn. During formal observations, the administrator focuses on what the teacher is doing, what the students are doing, and how well everyone is doing it. It is nearly impossible for the administrator to focus on student achievement and its relationship to teaching during a one-hour observation. However, when standardized test scores are gathered, student grades are tabulated, and parent requests are made for particular teachers, the teacher's effectiveness, which may be celebrated or called into question, becomes apparent.

Within the Collaborative Model, the teacher has the opportunity from the start to establish, document, and provide multiple indicators that demonstrate an understanding of the link between effective teaching and student performance and achievement. When goals related to anticipated student growth and development are determined, the teacher has the opportunity and responsibility to provide evidence of how well students are progressing in meeting these goals.

It is important to note that this approach differs considerably from the more traditional expression of learning objectives, such as, "For every month of instruction, the student will demonstrate one month's growth in reading as measured by a standardized test." Rather, the Collaborative Model suggests that when teachers and/or districts establish student learning goals or standards, design instruction intended to maximize students potential in meeting the goals or standards, assess performance authentically, and then evaluate the instructional approaches, both teaching and student performance improve.

To accommodate this category, a first grade teacher established a goal that all of her students would develop phonemic awareness by the end of first grade. Through a variety of methods including periodic scheduled observations of children's word play, rhyming, taped oral reading samples, and oral tests of phonemic awareness, the teacher documented the students' progress throughout the school year. Based upon her findings, she adjusted her reading instruction accordingly in order to provide more personalized systematic instruction for students making slower progress.

One high school teacher's approach to this category involved his determination to include more student self-reflection in his writing program. He began by reading current recommendations about writers' workshops, focusing on the "revision stage" of the writing process. Over a period of time the teacher modeled questions a writer might ask of a peer reviewer concerning the clarity and meaning of a piece of writing. Students then began entering peer or teacher conferences with their own reflective questions to guide the conversation about the piece. As a result, the teacher discovered that student writing improved, conferences became more productive and meaningful, and students had greater ownership of their writing. The teacher's insights about how students' self-assessment questions guided their revisions changed his teaching practices.

Contributions to School and Community

Setting goals for this category represents a new aspect of the educational field for many teachers. It broadens the reach of the teacher's influence and forges a connection between the classroom and community. The purpose of the category is to encourage teachers to actively involve themselves in the broader community by sharing their expertise and enthusiasm with parents and other community members.

Goals for this category may be quite diverse, idiosyncratic, and satisfying for the respective teacher. Examples include one teacher who worked to preserve a section of fragile wetlands near her home and school. Her fourth grade students joined her in learning about the birds that lived in the area and the few wetlands that serve as migratory havens for particular species. Her personal interest and commitment were transmitted to her students when the class invited an environmentalist and a developer to debate the merits of preserving the wetlands or offering them up for development. The teacher's decision to become involved in the community discussion led directly to assisting her students in weighing complex environmental issues.

Another teacher designed a plan to inform community parents about the value of reading aloud to children. She presented her plan to members of the parent-teacher organization and enlisted their support in developing a newsletter. Her project culminated with a community-wide Read-Aloud Celebration that was promoted in the press and on television. As a result, participants were better informed about and more actively engaged in the read-aloud process. This goal also engendered widespread attention and excitement for reading in the teacher's community.

Both of these teachers became involved in projects that had far-reaching effects. Projects on a smaller scale, such as pen-pal letter writing to the elderly in a local nursing home or chairing a membership committee for the local reading association also have merit in this category, which encourages teachers to become involved and make a difference in whatever is interesting and meaningful to them.

THE COLLABORATIVE MODEL PORTFOLIO PROCESS

The Collaborative Model of Teacher Evaluation is congruent with other portfolio processes recommended for elementary and secondary classrooms (Tierney, Carter, & Desai, 1991), as well as for preservice teachers in university teacher education courses (McLaughlin & Vogt, 1996). The Model is goal-based, multidimensional, involves multiple indicators, is authentic, personal, relevant, and directly linked to the curriculum. Further, the process is collaborative: It encourages participants to take an active role in their own growth and development, and it enables them to demonstrate what they know in ways that encompass their personal learning styles (Vogt, McLaughlin, & Ruddell, 1993). Finally, the process is compatible with current theories of learning and teaching because teachers (1) demonstrate their own meaning construction; (2) are involved in a collaborative process requiring interactions and support from peers and supervisors; (3) are nurtured through the inquiry process; (4) demonstrate growth in their teaching over time; and (5) reflect and self-assess, thus becoming reflective practitioners.

When using the Collaborative Model, it is important to remember that reflection and collaboration permeate the process. Participants reflect upon each goal, individual evidences, and the completed portfolio. Collaboration with team members begins in the professional development stage and continues through the portfolio evaluation. The combination of these factors establishes a climate of thoughtful collegiality and self-renewal.

The following steps are offered to facilitate use of the Collaborative Model.

- Endorsing the Model
- Establishing portfolio review teams
- Providing professional development in the portfolio process
- Drafting preliminary goals and descriptions of possible artifacts (Portfolio Planner)
- Holding initial portfolio conversations
- Writing a collaborative statement of goals for each category
- Collecting evidence
- Holding interim portfolio conversations
- Presenting the portfolio
- Completing the rubrics
- Holding the final portfolio conversation

Each of these steps is described below.

Endorsing the Collaborative Model

As those of us in education know, change is often slow, and there is occasional resistance to new ideas. However, throughout the country, assessment practices have been evolving, and portfolios are becoming widely used in classrooms and universities. While some educators have enthusiastically embraced the concept, others have been slower to accept this assessment innovation. Therefore, before implementing the Collaborative Model of Teacher Evaluation, all stakeholders must endorse the process. It is imperative that both faculty and administrators endorse the Model.

As a school or district begins using portfolios for teacher evaluation, it is advisable for a group to pilot the process rather than invoke a district-wide mandate. Teacher ownership is critical if the process is to be successful. Also, while collective bargaining agreements might not permit full-scale portfolio implementation at first, they might endorse a pilot project. As with any new idea in education, loyal supporters of the concept will be more likely to persuade others, and once the Model has been used and found to be successful, others may wish to participate.

One major decision that must be made early in the process is whether the period of evaluation is one, two, or three years. Yearly evaluation is required in nearly all districts for beginning teachers, but once tenured, many districts move to biannual or triannual formal evaluation. This is an important distinction because teachers' goals may be short-term and/or long-term and need to be written accordingly.

Establishing Portfolio Review Teams

Once a cohort of educators who support portfolios for teacher evaluation is established, a list of participants is disseminated. From this list, portfolio review teams are created. Teachers undergoing evaluation may recommend particular members they wish to include on their teams. These could be colleagues within their school and grade level, teachers selected across grade levels and schools, or administrators. While all team members serve as sources of collegial support, it is important that one of the teachers on the team be designated as a mentor, especially for beginning teachers. This person should be very familiar with the portfolio process and ideally should be selected by the teacher. At least one team member should be a site administrator.

Because team members will work together for one to three years, it is important that all feel comfortable about the process and believe they can enhance teacher growth and development through this type of evaluation. In addition to the teacher who is being evaluated, it is recommended that teams consist of at least one administrator and two other teachers. Team members may serve as evaluators for more than one teacher. Teams of more than five may prove unwieldy.

Providing Professional Development in the Portfolio Process

While all team members have committed to the portfolio process, not all may have the same level of expertise concerning this type of authentic assessment. Therefore, it is important that all stakeholders in the district who are associated with the Collaborative Model receive professional development in the principles and practices of portfolio assessment. These include the theories underpinning portfolios, what constitutes effective portfolio development in the schools, the role of reflection and collaboration, goal-setting, selecting artifacts, and the use of rubrics for portfolio review. Ideally, each team should have at least one member who actively uses portfolios for classroom assessment and who can serve as a resource in the process. The more team members know and understand about the process, the more likely the experience is to be positive for all involved.

Drafting Preliminary Goals

Drafting the preliminary goals depends, in part, on the experience of the teacher to be evaluated and the time frame required for accomplishing the goals. For beginning teachers, drafts of the goals may be sketchy and incomplete, and most will be short-term—that is, they can be accomplished within one school year. More experienced teachers may have clearer ideas about their personal goals for each category, and their goals may be detailed and ambitious, with the intent that they extend over several years. It is important that district standards and curriculum documents serve as guides for development and that attention is given to previous evaluation recommendations, if relevant.

The Portfolio Planner (see Figure I-2 and Appendix A) is used during the goal-drafting phase. A section of the Planner is completed for each category within the Collaborative Model, providing the teacher with an organizational framework for writing goals and selecting artifacts. Once preliminary goals are drafted, the teacher uses the Planner to list the artifacts that will be submitted to support each goal, along with a rationale for how the artifacts provide evidence of progress in attaining the respective goals. Used in this way, the Portfolio Planner provides the first opportunity for the teacher to reflect on why particular artifacts or evidences are selected to support personal goals. The teacher also generates a proposed timeline for accomplishing the goals.

It is important to note that the completion of the portfolio process is not intended to be competitive in any way. Rather, each teacher's personal goals will be idiosyncratic, unique to the teacher's interests, strengths, and abilities. However, there may be instances when two or more teachers may wish to collaborate on a particular goal, such as implementing team teaching or peer coaching. Obviously, this is one of the strengths of the process: It is individualistic, but also flexible. Once the teacher's preliminary goals have been drafted, it is time to hold the first portfolio conversation with other team members. Approximately two weeks before the conversation, the teacher distributes copies of the Portfolio Planner to all involved in the meeting. This can be accommodated through electronic mail to facilitate communication.

Collaborative Model Portfolio Planner
Individual Category

Category One: Educational Philosophy

Name _____ District _____

School _____ Portfolio from _____ to _____

- Please list your proposed evidences in the spaces provided. Use additional sheets if necessary.
- In your rationale statement, briefly explain how your
  evidence relates to the goal.
- Remember to share copies of your Portfolio Planner for
  each goal with all team members at least two weeks prior
  to your team meeting.

Goal:_____

_____

_____

Portfolio Possibilities:

1. _____

Rationale: _____

_____

2. _____

Rationale: _____

_____

(Adapted from McLauglin & Vogt, 1996)

Figure I-2   Portfolio Planner

Holding the Initial Portfolio Conversation with Team Members

During this initial meeting with the team, the teacher introduces his or her goals within each category and presents the Portfolio Planner. Team members respond by making suggestions, offering support and guidance, and reviewing the feasibility of accomplishing the goals. Any questions or concerns about the process are discussed, and the projected timeline for accomplishing the goals is introduced. At this time, team members serve as supportive advocates rather than critics, though it is important that they voice any reservations they have about the goals, artifacts, or timeline. The team may also wish to discuss how the goals across categories relate to each other, to district standards, and to curriculum documents. Some stakeholders may request that certain categories and the goals within them carry more weight or importance than others. Decisions such as these should be made during this initial conference.

The team reviews the rubrics that will be used by both the teacher and each team member to evaluate individual portfolio goals and the final portfolio. The criteria upon which the rubrics are based can be found in the Standards for Evaluation (see Figure I-3 and Appendix B). It is critically important that all team members understand the rubrics to assure consistency in their use, since reliability is central to the process. To facilitate the evaluation process, a rubric is completed by each team member for both individual goals and the completed portfolio (see Appendixes C and D). Some districts choose to adopt the rubric presented with the Collaborative Model, while others may elaborate on it to meet their particular needs.

During the initial portfolio conversation, the team sets dates for future conferences. This is especially important for beginning teachers who need more support and assistance and perhaps more conversations. It is the teacher's responsibility to take the suggestions from this first portfolio conversation into consideration when writing the final draft of the personal goals for each category.

Writing a Collaborative Statement of Goals for Each Category

Based on the information gleaned from the portfolio conversation, the teacher refines the goals for each category and finalizes the list of primary artifacts that will be used to demonstrate progress in meeting the goals. Because of the dynamic nature of the portfolio process, it is likely that other ideas for artifacts will come to mind once the process begins. These can be added to the original list, although the purpose here is not to collect everything that

Collaborative Model
Standards for Evaluation

4.0 Exceptional application and depth of self-reflection are demonstrated. Initiative, creativity, independence, diversity, and risk-taking are evident. Performances are totally professional in appearance and are congruent with portfolio goals.

3.0 Thorough application and depth of self-reflection are demonstrated. Performances are diverse. Performances are very professional in appearance and are congruent with portfolio goals.

2.0 Adequate application and depth of self-reflection are demonstrated. Performances are somewhat diverse. Performances are professional in appearance and are mostly congruent with portfolio goals.

1.0 Inadequate application and depth of self-reflection are demonstrated. There is little variety in performances. Performances are less than professional in appearance and are minimally congruent with portfolio goals.

Figure I-3   Standards for Evaluation

supports the goal. Rather, the teacher should purposefully choose those evidences that most clearly demonstrate his or her growth and development within each category.

The revised goals, proposed artifacts, and timeline are presented in writing to all team members. Team members, including the teacher, sign and date the document demonstrating consensus about the teacher's evaluation plan. This is an important step in the process because it protects the teacher from potential conflicts about the proposed goals and artifacts.

Collecting Evidence

The teacher may begin collecting artifacts as soon as consensus is reached about the goals. Because this type of assessment is ongoing and dynamic, it is strongly recommended to use a three-ring binder or other type of portfolio folder to store the evidences over time. Dividing the binder into sections representing each of the categories helps to organize the materials as they are gathered. This makes it much easier to reflect on each goal and each piece of evidence.

As the school year progresses, the teacher may find appropriate artifacts that were not identified on the Portfolio Planner. Of course, adding new evidences is encouraged because they demonstrate that the teacher is using the goals to guide planning and instruction.

Holding Interim Portfolio Conversations

While the beginning and ending portfolio conversations are integral parts of the process, it is often beneficial to call meetings of team members during the course of the year to discuss problems or assess progress. It is up to the individual teacher and/or team members to determine if and when additional portfolio conversations are necessary and what the agenda of these meetings will be. These conferences may be especially helpful for beginning teachers and for those experienced teachers for whom the portfolio process is new. With the availability and ease of electronic mail, interim conversations can easily occur on-line. This type of support, especially from the mentor, greatly enhances the portfolio experience for the teacher.

Occasionally, a teacher exhibiting teaching difficulties may be going through the portfolio process. Perhaps the administrator's observations have uncovered some problems with instruction or the mentor or other team members become aware of difficulties. In this case, portfolio conversations can serve as an opportunity for team members to provide support, assistance, and intervention, if needed. This may necessitate refocusing some of the goals to assist the teacher in working on areas needing improvement.

Presenting the Portfolio

At the end of the school year, whether the teacher is being reviewed yearly or biannually, all teachers involved in the portfolio process present their portfolios. Depending on the district process, this presentation can be public or it can be more private, with only the team members present. The purpose of the presentation is to have a collegial, supportive, and social celebration of the teacher's accomplishments during the year. The presentation is highly reflective for the teacher, and it provides an opportunity for personal goals to be examined in terms of accomplishments and progress. Artifacts are shared and discussed as the teacher talks about what has been learned, what is yet to be accomplished, and perhaps what roadblocks have prevented completion of some of the goals. The teacher's self-evaluation, based on the portfolio rubric, is also shared with the team. For the teacher on a multiyear review, he or she has the opportunity to review goals, make revisions, additions, or other changes prior to the beginning of the next year.

Completing the Rubric

At the conclusion of the portfolio presentation, each team member has the opportunity to review the portfolio. This generally occurs over a two-week period. Following this review, all team members complete the rubric. This involves indicating on a continuum how well the goals have been accomplished and writing a brief reflection about the teacher's performance. The Collaborative Model's Standards for Evaluation and reproducible rubric forms for individual goals and the completed portfolio are included in Appendixes B, C, and D, respectively.

Holding the Final Portfolio Conversation

During a final portfolio conversation, the completed rubrics and comments are shared with the teacher. The teacher then has the opportunity to respond either in writing or in conversation with the administrator and other team members. This final conversation also serves as a catalyst for the generation of new or revised goals within each category. These goals will serve as the foundation for the following year's teaching and assessment process.

The preceding steps are recommended as guidelines for implementing the portfolio process for teacher evaluation. It is important to remember that any evaluation process must have consistency (reliability), and it must represent an authentic and accurate picture of the teacher's teaching performance (validity). Therefore, whatever evaluation process a district adopts, it should be designed carefully and thoughtfully. Though portfolio assessment is by definition highly flexible, uniformity in the process helps to ensure fairness for all its stakeholders.

EXAMPLES OF TEACHERS' GOALS AND ARTIFACTS

In order to illuminate the portfolio process more fully, the following goals and artifacts are offered as examples of what five teachers chose to submit as evidence of their teaching effectiveness. The examples span each category of the Collaborative Model. The teachers represent a variety of grade levels from elementary to high school, and they range in experience from a relatively new teacher (three years of experience) to a veteran of nearly twenty years. Two of the teachers are working in California; the other three teach in Pennsylvania.

It is interesting to note that several of the teachers' personal goals extend beyond one category. This is common because of the overlap between a teacher's desire to learn something new at the same time he or she may be attempting to implement the new learning in the classroom. Also, the goals presented here represent only one of several goals that each teacher would submit during a year's time. These goals and the artifacts that support them are representative of the diversity found when teachers are encouraged to set goals for themselves.

Educational Philosophy

Debbie Stinner has been teaching for ten years. Within the past three years, her school's name changed from "junior high school" to "middle school." Along with the name change came many of the reform efforts found in current research about middle schools, including interdisciplinary instruction, team teaching, thematic units, longer periods of time for instruction, "families" or units, core classes (e.g., social studies and English), and exploratory electives. These proposed changes resulted in many discussions about middle school education. These in turn caused Debbie to rethink and ultimately articulate her philosophy of teaching young adults.

Debbie's teacher training had been in elementary education, yet middle school youngsters' needs are far different from those of elementary school students. While learning about the middle school reform movement, she found that her own notions about teaching and learning were undergoing a significant change. Even though Debbie had always considered her classroom to be "student-centered," she came to realize that middle school reform required teachers to release a great deal of responsibility for learning to the students themselves. Her role became more of a facilitator and moderator as her school gradually changed from a junior high school with six class periods taught by six teachers to interdisciplinary block classes that were taught by a "unit" of teachers who team taught.

For the category of Educational Philosophy, Debbie wrote about the philosophical changes in teaching that came about as a result of her becoming a student of the middle school reform effort. Though she says this philosophical statement is still a work in progress, writing it down helped Debbie ground her new feelings about middle school education in the realities of her everyday teaching.

Curriculum and Instruction

As a result of her philosophical evolution, Debbie and her unit team decided to focus on team teaching and cross-curricular activities as a curriculum and instruction goal. They were challenged, along with the other three teams in the school, to create one cross-curricular unit within the first two years of the school being renamed as a middle school. Their dream was to form a truly cross-curricular unit, one that would tie together all five content areas. This goal became the focus of her curricular changes in the new middle school, and the artifacts that Debbie submitted for the portfolio all supported the creation of the cross-curricular theme.

The science teacher, a member of Debbie's team, conceived the idea of their unit: World War II. The teachers on the team enthusiastically embraced the theme and started expanding on the science teacher's original ideas almost immediately. Debbie stated in her portfolio submission that although the teachers did have disagreements during their meetings, time was also spent laughing together and sharing ideas.

The team of teachers aimed to foster student teamwork by grouping students on projects related to the World War II theme. To accomplish this, the teachers from diverse content areas created a "schedule-free week" in which students worked with their teams on their selected projects with a supervising teacher. During this week, students were not required to be in certain rooms at certain times, a drastic change from the normally rigid bell schedule. They were allowed to use a coupon from their ration books to take a break in the Canteen (the reading classroom renamed for the project), listen to some Big Band sounds, and be served "pop" and chips by parent volunteers. When the unit was completed, the respective supervising teacher evaluated the final team project. The grade earned by the students on the project applied to each subject area.

As a result of the success of this cross-disciplinary unit, the teaching team planned a new unit on Justice in America. This unit, tied the judicial system (history and literature) to the measurements and physics (math and science) involved in a bus accident scheduled to go to trial. This once again required the input and dedication of all the content teachers in Debbie's team. By the end of the year, Debbie's colleagues and their students had contributed to turning a traditional junior high into a reformed, exciting middle school. Debbie in her reflections stated the "birth of the cross-curricular unit was not without labor pains," but the end result was definitely worth all the work.

Professional Development

For this category, Muntzi Verga, a fifth grade teacher, established a goal to implement literature discussion circles in her classroom in order to develop the students' comprehension and teamwork. However, she knew very little about how to organize, manage, and evaluate student performance in the discussion circles. Though she heard teachers talking about the process and read articles about discussion circles in teaching magazines and educational journals, Muntzi still felt unprepared to establish the discussion circles in her own classroom.

So, Muntzi wrote a professional development plan for learning more about discussion circles. She contacted a former professor who directed her to an International Reading Association publication on discussion (Gambrell & Almasi, 1996), which she read. She read another helpful book on how to organize discussion circles (Daniels, 1994), which was recommended by her colleagues. She also signed up for a weekend workshop on the approach and attended it with a friend.

The first step in Muntzi's professional development was to define what literature discussion circles are:

In literature circles, students are becoming inspired, self-directed learners and team players as they participate in discussion groups of four or five readers. The students choose literature books and groups are formed around their choices. They assign themselves pages to read, rotate roles, and meet regularly to discuss their books. The groups are student run and the teacher is a facilitator (Verga, 1997).

From this definition, Muntzi created an implementation plan based upon what she had learned. She typed group member responsibilities, created and laminated group task charts, created a literature response chart for discussion questions, and wrote a preferences checklist and post-discussion self-assessment instrument for the fifth graders. Following Daniels' recommendations, she created group assessments as well as a teacher assessment plan. She also reorganized the classroom literature books into various categories according to genre and topic. She read an article on "book talks" and began "advertising" literature books with her students.

At this point, Muntzi's plan also became a goal for the portfolio category, Curriculum and Instruction, because she began implementing literature discussion circles in her classroom. She introduced the process to her students, explaining the various roles the students would assume (Discussion Director, Artful Artist, Word Finder, Passage Picker, Connector). She had the students complete their preference assessment, and then they began. Throughout the first semester of implementation, Muntzi made modifications and adjustments to the program as the children became more comfortable with discussion circles. By the second semester, literature discussion was a regular part of Muntzi's reading curriculum.

In the spring of the program's first year, Muntzi was asked to present a workshop for her school district on literature discussion. She shared with her colleagues the success stories from her classroom as well as her organizational and management plans. The response was very positive, and as Muntzi began the process with a new group of children the following year, her confidence soared. The following May, Muntzi presented her literature discussion ideas and techniques in a research symposium sponsored by the county department of education.

Would Muntzi have implemented literature discussion in her classroom without the formal process of identifying a plan for professional development? Perhaps, but from Muntzi's perspective, the district validated and supported her efforts more because the changes she was making in her classroom were consistent with her stated professional development goals. She doubts the district would have approved the two days she was released from school to attend her first discussion workshop and then later to present a workshop. This successful, creative teacher is now determining her future professional development plans because her earlier goals have been thoroughly accomplished. Literature discussion circles are now an accepted and important aspect of Muntzi's balanced literacy program.

Another example of a goal established for the category of Professional Development concerns the work of Robin Andress, an elementary school teacher. Her school district had a stated objective of providing elementary school students with a variety of experiences that integrate technology with instruction. To attain her goal of improving her professional growth, Robin decided she needed to learn more about computer technology. In writing her professional development goal, she stated, "This goal is encouraging me to become more familiar with different types of technology and what they can be used for in and outside the classroom."

Robin began by enrolling in a graduate reading course that required the use of technology. She decided to learn how to use a presentation software program so that she could graphically present the Sub-Strata Factor Theory of Reading. She attended district-sponsored inservice sessions and received support from colleagues who were avid computer users. She stated they were "patient and helpful, encouraging me to become computer literate." In her reflections, Robin writes that although previously she was unable to even turn a computer on, she now knows how to write memos, build charts, use word processing, access the Internet, and present a video slide show. She concludes with, "I am now able to share these new skills with my students as well as colleagues. I will continue my computer growth through inservice and graduate classes. I know I will be a life-long learner when it comes to the many changes in computers."

Student Growth

Rosemary De Trolio took an interesting approach to this goal, which ultimately overlapped with other portfolio categories. Rosemary's goal was to create an extensive thematic plan that she would share with her third-grade team members. She first decided to volunteer as a mentor for a newly credentialed teacher who was hired to teach her grade level, third grade. The three women with whom she was working had varied experience: One was the first-year teacher, one woman had four years of experience, and the other had taught fifth grade for five years. Since Rosemary was most familiar with the third grade curriculum, she began researching and gathering ideas they all could use for the theme "Celebrate Hawaii." She collected books, materials, photos, videos, and some personal items she had found when traveling on the islands. She ultimately decided to concentrate the theme on four areas of study: Each teacher would develop an area of study within her own class-room. Rosemary planned to facilitate a culminating celebration of Hawaii with the children and families of all four classes.

Rosemary's class researched the topic of travel and tourism. Her third graders studied famous places, animals, plants, culture, dance, and food of the islands. They made travel posters, wrote advertisements, and served as tour guides at the Hawaiian Day celebration. Another class studied the flora and fauna of Hawaii, and with Rosemary's list of animals and plants as well as a real Hibiscus, pineapple, and creeper vine, they were able to study the plants in depth. This class made Macaws, five-foot palm trees, and animal dioramas. The third teacher was interested in having her class explore volca-noes. She had her students build and explode volcanoes. Rosemary supplied her with posters, information sheets, and other materials for classroom use.

Rosemary spent the most time assisting the first-year teacher who chose to have her students study Hawaiian dance and culture. She shared Hawaiian music, Luau facts and ideas, information about dress, books, and photos. To share what they learned through the theme, the children sang and danced and incorporated many connections with family, home, and the early culture of Hawaii.

The research, project making, and text study took four weeks. Rosemary stated that by the time the classes were ready for the celebration, the children were "living and breathing Hawaiian." Rosemary created "tropical" writing paper for the classes to use for designing parent invitations as well as thank-you notes for the parent volunteers. Food donations included ham, fruits, and juices. The final celebration, held in the school's decorated gym, was at-tended by approximately 150 children and parents, many dressed as Hawai-ian tourists. The local newspaper covered the event that was judged by all to be an enormous success. As Rosemary described it, "I think that the most wonderful part of this was the pure excitement and joy the children experi-enced. They really learned so much and did a fantastic job. I was so fortu-nate, too, to work with wonderful creative teachers who took the information and elaborated, created, and extended it in their own way." At the conclusion of her portfolio submission, Rosemary included photographs of the culmi-nating celebration.

Contributions to School and Community

Contributing to school and community is a new type of professional commitment for most teachers, and many choose to design goals that not only contribute to the community, but also enhance the learning of their students. Such was the goal designed by Patty Clark, an experienced Title I teacher in a large urban high school. As the coordinator of her school's Title I program, Patty saw many students who were unsuccessful in content courses because of weak reading, writing, and study skills. Though she attempted to help her students with these problems, many continued to do poorly in classes and were at serious risk of dropping out of school.

At the same time, at a nearby university, secondary preservice teachers were enrolled in a required reading methods course. A field-work component for this class involved a tutorial component in which students must spend 12–15 hours tutoring middle or high school students who have delayed literacy development. Patty had helped a few of these tutors by placing them for their field work with some of her students.

For her goal in Contributions to Community, Patty decided to create a tutoring program involving the university students and local high school students. She met with district and school administrators and with the professors who taught the secondary reading methods course at the university to discuss her plan and seek their support. She then involved a large number of content area teachers from her school who would be willing to release students from their classes to work with university tutors for two days a week. At first, there was some resistance to the plan, since the teachers had little information about what the high school students would be learning during this time. Therefore, Patty and the professor worked together to ensure that the university students would be prepared to make this a meaningful learning experience for the adolescents needing help.

After receiving initial support from all those involved, Patty established a tutoring schedule, created volunteer tutor nametags and informational packets, and began soliciting high school students who were willing to work with the preservice teachers. At first, only a few responded and completed the 12-week program. However, the word quickly spread and students began coming to Patty seeking assistance.

At present, the collaborative partnership between the university and the high school is working exceptionally well. Each semester, between 30 and 60 university students tutor the high school students, many of whom are English language learners. The preservice teachers learn about assessment, planning, instruction, and evaluation; the high school students learn reading, writing, and study strategies. Patty's program has been recognized as an exemplary model of school–university collaboration.

All of these examples illustrate that when teachers are given the opportunity to design meaningful, personally relevant goals for their own growth and development, their students also benefit. The performances presented here are typical of the kinds of activities and projects that teachers have undertaken. In the next section, teachers and administrators reflect on the Collaborative Model and its effect on their teaching, learning, and development.

PART THREE: REACTIONS TO THE COLLABORATIVE MODEL OF TEACHER EVALUATION

As with other innovative practices, there have been positive responses to the Collaborative Model, and there have also been some concerns. To document reactions to the Model, teachers and administrators from school districts in three states responded to a survey (N=126). We share their reactions with you to facilitate the use of the Model in your district.

When discussing whether they preferred to be evaluated solely through traditional types of observation or through the Collaborative Model, 100% of the teachers and 98% of the administrators chose the Collaborative Model. One hundred percent of the teachers and administrators agreed that administrators should also maintain performance portfolios based on the Collaborative Model. One hundred percent of the teachers and administrators endorsed the value of portfolio conversations as an integral part of the evaluation process. Responses to specific questions, examples of teacher-generated goals, and sample evidences are included in this section.

STRENGTHS OF THE COLLABORATIVE MODEL OF TEACHER EVALUATION

Teachers and administrators were asked to discuss what they viewed as specific strengths of the Collaborative Model. The following strengths were identified most frequently:

- It addresses the strengths and weaknesses of novice as well as veteran teachers.

- It is situated, dynamic, multifaceted, and ongoing.
- It values teacher and administrator self-reflection.
- It affords teachers an opportunity to "practice what they preach" in their classrooms.
- Goal-setting offers direction to teacher growth.
- Self-goal-setting allows teachers to address personal areas of need and/or interest.
- Educators have ownership of the process.
- Participants view themselves as constructivists.
- It reinforces the current practice of mentors and peer coaches.
- It doesn't exclude observation by administrators or peers. It broadens the lens.
- It redefines the teacher/administrator relationship.
- It is an impetus for continued growth and self-renewal.

When commenting on the strengths of the Collaborative Model, both teachers and administrators offered enthusiastic endorsement. To document this, samples of detailed responses from teachers and administrators are quoted.

Teacher Reactions:

> The strengths of the Collaborative Model are self-set goals, account-ability for the attainment of goals, and peer interaction. Teachers are bombarded with ideas to try out in the classroom. We are encouraged to do hands-on science, integration of technology, integrated language arts, multiple intelligences, learning styles, cooperative learning, music, art, problems solving. . . . The list is endless. However, being mere mortals, there is no way for teachers to address all of these issues in a quality manner. By setting annual or bi-annual goals in various areas, teachers can be more directed in the work they are doing. And with the guidance of administration and peers in reaching these goals, more quality work can be accomplished in each area.

> I like the goal setting component followed by the action plan. Not only does this direct the teacher, but ideas are put in place to make it happen. I also appreciate the reflection process and making connections to what we are doing. This makes our teaching more meaningful and encourages risk-taking.

I believe all of the components are critical for a well-rounded educator. Specifically, I like the school and community component. I view the interaction patterns between the school, home and community as extremely important for future life skills. By valuing the community, we teach our children about the value of cooperation.

Administrator Reactions:

There are many strengths of the Collaborative Model. The very fact that the teacher sets her own professional goals gives her ownership of the process. It also gives her direction for many inservice conferences throughout the year, classroom projects, professional readings as well as the set up of her classroom management and style of teaching. Too often, teachers attend conferences on a "one shot" topic which often serve as a validation of present instruction but does little to change direction of that instruction. The opportunity for matching teachers with similar portfolio directions, offers a productive direction for district/building inservices as well as professional resources. Informal classroom observations by the building administrator also become more meaningful because more than a well-delivered lesson is evaluated. The progress of the chosen goal can be observed. Measuring student growth with the Collaborative Model takes on more meaning. The assessment can better match the method of instruction. Instead of having a non-related assessment handed down which used a "hit or miss" mode of assessing students, the assessment more accurately measures just what the teacher is trying to teach. The Contributions to School and Community component adds relevancy to what is being learned in the classroom. No longer will subjects be taught for the purpose of individual mastery. Instead, the impact of how learning can be used and related to the students' life experiences will motivate students to achieve.

The strengths of this model are its framework for exhibiting concrete examples of growth in terms of instructional design, professional knowledge, and reflection on an actual educational philosophy. Also, teachers get to conference with the administrator and peers based on already established goals. Simply by forcing teachers to reflect on their strengths and weaknesses and how they affect students, this process is light years ahead of the old observation-conference model.

COLLABORATIVE MODEL OF TEACHER EVALUATION VERSUS TRADITIONAL OBSERVATION

When commenting on the value of using the Collaborative Model rather than observation alone, teachers and administrators found that the Model views the evaluation process through a broader lens, offering a fuller, more multi-faceted view of the teacher. Other thoughts expressed by the survey participants include the following:

Teachers:

> The Collaborative Model is a much better view of teacher performance. It includes the unobservable thought processes behind the observable actions and activities within the classroom. It also offers a portrait of a teacher as a human being as well as a professional.

> An observation records only one point in time in the school year. The picture is limited, sketchy and often superficial. The Collaborative Model happens over time and requires forethought, choice, planning and implementation by the teacher, probably with administrative input. The picture of the teacher's thinking, efforts and work is much more visible and complete.

Administrators:

> Annual observations are so limiting in their ability to assess the true capabilities of a teacher. It is only one dimensional. Often times, the success of the observation is based on the creativity and organization of the lesson being observed. It gives limited background as to how a teacher thinks, what she values and where she is headed. It is almost as if she is reading a script from a well written lesson plan which could have been taken directly from the teacher's guide. After the observation, the administrator leaves knowing whether the teacher is an accomplished performer rather than a committed educator.

> As your research indicates a one time (or even two or three time) observation system only gives a limited snapshot of a teacher's strengths and weaknesses. There is also little room for goal setting, reflection and conferencing. Any conferences that result from the observation model usually build on something negative observed during the visit. In most cases no process of constructive goal setting and analytical reflection based on these goals occurs.

ADMINISTRATORS MAINTAINING PORTFOLIOS

Teachers and administrators also shared their thinking about administrators creating portfolios based upon the Collaborative Model. Both groups valued administrators' active participation in the process.

Teachers:

> Administrators need to understand the evaluation process, and I can think of no better way to understand it than participate in it.

> After studying and using portfolios, I feel they provide a complete picture of a person's performance, whether the person is a second grade student, a tenured teacher, or the school superintendent. Portfolios are the most efficient vehicle to set and work toward the attainment of reasonable goals. And only in setting and attaining these goals will performance increase.

Administrators:

> I believe administrators should be doing this whether or not teachers are. Administrators are evaluated on snapshots of performance much less than the typical 30–45 minutes of official observation that happens with teachers in classrooms! Very few administrators have daily access to their supervisors the way teachers have access to their principals. If any group of educators is short changed on actual performance observations, it is administrators. A portfolio would allow the administrator to highlight areas where much time and effort have been expended which may not be known by anyone else. It is a great opportunity for a principal to demonstrate the broad range of responsibilities and issues with which he/she deals. Also, district level (central office) administrators can profile their unique roles in this format and share the information with building level leadership to allow them a glimpse of the diverse and demanding centralized tasks.

> Modeling is a major tool in helping people to understand a framework or a concept. It can only help. Also administrators would be more empathetic to the process that they are asking teachers to take part in. If administrators feel comfortable with the process and the pieces of evidence that they are asked to provide and reflect on, then they will be more successful in working through this process with their teachers.

PORTFOLIO CONVERSATIONS

Part of the performance portfolio process involves portfolio conversations in which teachers and administrators interact. When considering this aspect of the Collaborative Model, both teachers and administrators noted the value of this part of the process.

Teachers:

> Without that interaction the portfolio would be diminished. As with student portfolios, it is the dialogue that accompanies the sharing that imbues it with so much meaning.

> Portfolio conversations are a very important part of the process. They allow for an exchange rather than just agreement, or disagreement, with the administrator's observations.

> I feel it is important for all educators to interact. The school should work as a team, all people sharing professional growth. The school needs to be a community where all are free to take risks and support each other.

Administrators:

> Without such portfolio conversations, there is no true self-reflection of the evaluation process. Merely perusing the content or write-up of the portfolio could not possibly offer insight into how the teacher actually benefited from the experience. The highs and lows of the process need to be discussed. Direction for future portfolio experiences is also invaluable. The portfolio conversation also provides a stage for teachers to share their pride in their accomplishments. One can also view the portfolio conversation as an accountability tool. If a teacher is explaining and discussing what was accomplished, this would be difficult to do without having truly experienced all of what was written down.

> Conferencing is central to any portfolio process. Without conferencing it becomes just another exercise in paper management and paper pushing. The conference that is built on goals and reflection will be a meaningful process that will force the administrator and the teacher to address deeper and more important educational issues.

TEACHER AND ADMINISTRATOR CONCERNS ABOUT THE COLLABORATIVE MODEL

While a vast majority of the responses to the survey focused on positive attributes of the Collaborative Model, concerns about its implementation and use were also recorded. The following issues were those most frequently cited by teachers and administrators.

- Time is a factor for implementation, portfolio development, and portfolio conversations.

- Reflection is a key element in the process. It is critical that participants understand how to reflect on various aspects of their performance.

- This procedure should be included in the collective bargaining agreement.

- While most teachers and administrators embraced the concept from the outset, it is important to assure that each individual understands how the process works and the degree of ownership each teacher maintains.

Teachers:

"This is time-consuming;"

"It's important to know that the local district can make choices about the timeline;"

"All involved need to know how to use reflection in beneficial ways;"

"I believe teachers should be able to add categories. I am a poet and my writing life colors my practice."

Administrators:

"The time required is certainly greater than the present system. However, the meaningful outcomes are well worth the time investment;"

"Making sure that teachers understand that this is an outgrowth of the classroom portfolio system and a viable tool for evaluating growth over a long period of time is an extremely important concept."

The concerns noted by the teachers and administrators are addressed in a question and answer format (see Appendix E).

PART FOUR:
TEACHER-GENERATED
PORTFOLIO GOALS AND EVIDENCES

Part Four presents individual goals and sample evidence teachers have set within each category of the Model. The diversity of the goals and evidence reflects the idiosyncratic nature of the portfolio process. It is important to note that the artifacts presented in this section are only samples taken from multiple evidences teachers included to support each goal.

Since the Collaborative Model is integrated, some topics may appear in goal statements for more than one category. For example, a teacher may wish to improve curriculum and instruction by incorporating portfolio assessment, but such a goal would also directly impact how student growth was documented.

Educational Philosophy

The goals in this category address the creation of educational philosophy statements as well as manifestations of the beliefs. Many teachers stated that their philosophical perspectives have changed over time; many also reported that they really hadn't thought about their philosophy for many years. This category provided focus and motivation for contemplating their philosophical stance.

Cooperative Learning   To create a classroom which incorporates cooperative learning partners. Sample Evidence: Lesson plans, photos and videotapes, student reflective journal entries.

Early Intervention   To learn more about Reading Recovery as it impacts my grade level. Sample Evidence: Reflective journal including reactions to professional publications and observations of and conversations with Reading Recovery teachers.

Facilitating   To become more of a facilitator than a director. Sample Evidence: Documentation of children taking a more active role during instruction.

Flexibility in Delivering Curriculum
To become increasingly more flexible in my delivery of the curriculum. Sample Evidence: Video segments of one theme in reading.

Inclusion
To write and implement a new educational philosophy reflecting the cooperative nature of teaching in an inclusionary setting. Sample Evidence: The philosophical statement, peer observations, and journal entries.

Individual Student Needs
To create a classroom atmosphere in which the pace of the curriculum presented can be adapted to meet the needs of every child. This includes the use of flexible grouping, adapted curriculum, and portfolio assessment. Sample Evidence: Student portfolios.

Inquiry-Based (Student-Generated) Curriculum
To employ constructivism to foster inquiry-based learning and student-generated curriculum. Sample Evidence: Videotapes, student portfolios, and changes in curriculum.

Learning Styles
To create a center-based learning environment that accommodates students' learning styles. Sample Evidence: Descriptions of learning centers, Videotapes of students with diverse learning styles using the centers.

Mentoring
To become a mentor for a novice teacher and develop a mentoring program for experienced students to serve as mentors to students who are new to our school. Sample Evidence: Reflective journal entries from participants and videotape of a "Meet My Mentor" celebration.

Motivation
To create an environment in which all children learn and enjoy learning. Sample Evidence: Videotapes that depict the learning environment and student reactions.

Multiple Intelligences	To integrate Gardner's theories about intelligence in my teaching. Sample Evidence: Student profiles of strengths in the seven areas.
Parental Understanding of Educational Philosophy	To help parents understand our philosophy with regard to reading. Sample Evidence: Newsletter developed from conferences and workshops I have attended and at which I have presented.
Peer Editing	To develop a structure for peer-editing. Sample Evidence: Samples of student work before and after editing and taped conversations about the experience the children had.
Philosophical Change	To update my philosophy regularly based on reality therapy. Sample Evidence: Reflective journal including rationale for change and how it impacts my teaching.
Professional Development	To develop a staff development plan that would encourage teachers to view our district's reading program as more inclusive than the literature anthology. Sample Evidence: Written observations of teachers who use other literature, creation of author-genre studies, and development of mini-lessons based on student need.
Professional Growth	To maintain active membership in a professional organization and read professional journals on a regular basis. Sample Evidence: Double-entry journal.
Response-Centered Classroom	To create a motivating, stimulating, noncoercive environment in which children will learn and feel successful. Sample Evidence: Written observations of students over time.
Student-Centered Learning	To maintain a child-centered focus that stresses all children will learn and do learn in different ways over a period of time. Sample Evidence: Improved student learning and active involvement.

Student-Centered Reading Support Program	To design a student-centered reading support program with the aim of encouraging student growth. Sample Evidence: Students' self-reflections about their progress.
Technology	To further integrate computer and related technology in my classroom. Sample Evidence: Projects from classes attended in multimedia and technological integration and applications in my teaching.
Theoretical Documentation of Educational Philosophy	To research and report the theoretical underpinnings of my educational philosophy. Sample Evidence: Research journal entries and reflections.
Writing	To create more opportunities for writing as a component of the reading curriculum. Sample Evidence: Materials created from workshop activities.
Writing a Personal Educational Philosophy	To examine my personal beliefs by writing and reflecting upon my educational philosophy. Sample Evidence: The written document and videotapes of how various beliefs are personified in my classroom.

Professional Development

Goals for professional development have ranged from attending workshops to reading professional journals, accessing technological resources, attending graduate classes, and sharing knowledge as presenters at professional conferences. This category offers teachers a place to plan and record their professional growth. Many participants have noted that prior to developing this goal, their professional development was a series of isolated incidences. Creating personal goals within this category not only motivates teachers to have a professional development plan, but also invites them to design it.

Computer Literacy   To become more fluent with the computer's capabilities. Sample Evidence: Reflections about professional development seminars attended and journal articles read.

Conflict Resolution   To increase my understanding of the process of conflict resolution. Sample Evidence: Observation of teachers using this concept, reflective journal, inservice sessions.

Continued Professional Development   To stay current in all areas of literacy education. Sample Evidence: Attend workshops, give workshops, read and reflect upon professional journal articles.

Emergent Literacy   To attend inservices and increase my knowledge of early literacy education. Sample Evidence: Videotapes of implementing emergent literacy strategies in my teaching.

Hemisphericity   To increase my knowledge of right and left brain thinking. Sample Evidence: Create activities that are specifically designed for left brain or right brain dominance.

Innovative Practice   To increase my knowledge of innovative practice by attending graduate classes. Sample Evidence: A portfolio of my course work from the classes.

Internet	To become more knowledgeable about the appropriate use of the internet in schools. Sample Evidence: Courses taken, projects created.
Journal Writing	To increase my knowledge of using journal writing across the curriculum, especially in math. Sample Evidence: Samples of children's journal writing across the curriculum.
Learning Styles	To integrate learning styles in my teaching. Sample Evidence: Materials made, observations of student use, developmentally appropriate activities, readings, discussions, record of activities and results.
Multiple Intelligences	To integrate multiple intelligences theory in my teaching. Sample Evidence: Lesson plans and videotapes.
Poetry Writing	To learn how to teach poetry writing. Sample Evidence: Poetry workshop materials, students' poems.
Portfolio Assessment	To broaden my knowledge of portfolio assessment. Sample Evidence: Portfolio from graduate class on this topic.
Professional Reading in Mathematics	To read more professional journals/books relating to grade level in math/reading instruction. Sample Evidence: Double-entry journal.
Quality School Theory	To become immersed in Quality School Theory, form an acceptance of it, and find a comfort zone which allows me to utilize the theory better in the classroom. Sample Evidence: Reflective journal entries based on workshops attended and professional journals.
Revision Stage of Writing Process	To make the revision process of writing more interesting/important to third and fourth graders. Sample Evidence: Attending workshops on teaching revision and sharing ideas with other teachers.

Rubrics	To learn to create and use rubrics. Sample Evidence: Students' reflective statements, display of products and rubrics.
Site-Based Management	To learn more about the tenets of Site-Based Management. Sample Evidence: Reflections on workshops attended and professional articles read.
Student Authors	To attend workshops specifically geared to writing in order to create more opportunities for student authors. Sample Evidence: Materials designed from workshop activities.
Team Planning	To develop sources for enhancing team planning. Sample Evidence: Bibliography of books and magazines and a list of teachers to use as mentors.
Technological Multimedia	Increase my knowledge and use of the various types of technological multimedia. Sample Evidence: Reactions to workshops, lesson plans using technological multi-media, student reactions.
Writing Workshop	To become more proficient in running a "Writer's Workshop" by attending a course on it. Sample Evidence: Videotapes, samples of student process work.

Curriculum and Instruction

A number of teachers noted that this category reminded them of the daily importance of curriculum. When processes such as the Collaborative Model are not ongoing, curriculum sometimes becomes an issue that is reworked every five years to accommodate long range planning. With its inclusion in the Model, it becomes a common focus.

Goals within this category reflect teachers as researchers, authors, and models. Teachers and students take active roles in each goal, whether engaging in center-based learning or integrating technology into the curriculum.

Active Learning	To create more of a hands-on classroom. Sample Evidence: Descriptions of centers, videotapes of students.
Assessment Systems	To develop more systematic means to assess (reading/math) progress in a more consistent manner. Sample Evidence: Checklists, rubrics, and artifacts.
Authoring Professional Articles	To write articles about what works best in my classroom. Sample Evidence: The articles, videotapes of the students as teachers.
Center-Based Learning	To update center-based techniques especially in science. Sample Evidence: Hard copies of e-mails with teachers who are more experienced in the teaching of science, videotapes of the students working in the centers.
Early Intervention Techniques	To incorporate Reading Recovery techniques into my teaching of first graders. Sample Evidence: Videotape of a lesson using a cut-up sentence, magnetic letters, dictated sentence, personal reflections, or peer observations.
Core Computer Lessons	To develop core lessons integrating the computer that could be used at various instructional levels. Sample Evidence: Copies of lesson plans, videotapes of students learning in content areas with the use of the computer, reflection.

Cross-Age Creative Problem Solving	Creative problem solving in a cross-age context. Sample Evidence: Videotape of my eighth grade students teaching younger students, students' reflective journal entries.
Developmentally Appropriate Practices	To use developmentally appropriate practices that challenge children to learn and to reach their developmental potential. Sample Evidence: Student portfolios.
Improved Spelling	To improve spelling in daily writing. Sample Evidence: Samples of children's writing, attending workshops.
Innovative Curriculum	To be involved in implementing and creating new ideas for Curriculum and Instruction. Sample Evidence: The curriculum, visitations to other schools.
Integrated Curriculum	To integrate science and social studies units to allow the children to see the relationship between the humanities and science. Sample Evidence: Bibliography of thematic materials, videotapes of students.
Internet	To explore and develop projects within the curriculum in which the internet will be integrated. Sample Evidence: Project description, downloaded disk of information, student portfolios.
Modifying Materials	To create more modifications for students in a heterogeneous classroom. Sample Evidence: Instructional frameworks for extension books.
	To provide a choice of reading material on various themes on all reading levels. Sample Evidence: Bibliography of classroom library materials by category.
Motivation	To motivate my students to learn by making changes to existing instructional materials. Sample Evidence: Students' reflections, observations.

Multiple Intelligences	To incorporate teaching to all intelligences in my units. Sample Evidence: Photographs and videotapes of children using multiple intelligences.
Pen Pal E-Mail Network	To establish a classroom program where primary-age children can pen pal on a computer network. Sample Evidence: Hard copies of e-mail correspondence, students' reactions to process.
Student-Generated Themes	To encourage the creation of a student-generated theme. Sample Evidence: Videotapes, written copy of theme.
Technology to Teach Report Writing	Use computers more effectively in the classroom especially for writing. Sample Evidence: Student reports and reflections on the process.
Thematic Instruction	To create thematic units with other professionals teaching at my grade level. Sample Evidence: Written copies of the units, teacher reflections on the process.

Student Growth

A multifaceted concept of student growth is reflected in teachers' goal-setting in this category. Educators want their students to experience academic, personal, and social progress during the school year.

Active Learners
To encourage students to become active learners in a risk-free environment. Sample Evidence: Kid-watching, record keeping.

Awareness of Academic Growth
To assist students in being more self-aware of academic growth and their best modes of learning. Sample Evidence: Student self-evaluations and anecdotal notes.

Collaboration
To help students become more collaborative through cooperative learning activities. Sample Evidence: Observations, student self-reflections.

Love of Reading
To encourage children to love reading and writing and to choose to engage in literacy activities independently. Sample Evidence: Book log, student writing.

Nonreaders
To teach second grade nonreaders to read. Sample Evidence: Informal assessments such as strategy use, writing samples, audiotapes of students reading.

Observations
To keep an annotated book of observations for each student with entries noting strengths and needs. Sample Evidence: The record book.

Problem-Solving
To help students learn to be better personal and academic problem solvers. Sample Evidence: Student problem-solving performances.

Reading Fluency
To increase reading fluency. Sample Evidence: Audiotape of individual students monthly reading.

Responsibility   To encourage students to take more responsibility for their interactions with peers. Sample Evidence: Observations of students working cooperatively, student self-reflections.

Self-Esteem   To assist students in feeling successful in what they do and to help them realize that they are important (self-worth). Sample Evidence: Entries from student reflective journals.

Student Choice   To incorporate student choice in more lessons. Sample Evidence: Sample lesson plans, observations, student reactions.

Students' Personal Bests   To enable each child to do his/her own personal best. Sample evidence: His/her portfolio.

Student Role in Assessment   I would like to encourage students to be more involved in assessing growth. Sample Evidence: Student self-assessments.

Technology   To enable students to access information on computers and use various technologies to produce projects. Sample Evidence: Audiotapes of students discussing project ideas and the role technology plays in project implementation.

Contributions to School and Community

This category offers teachers an opportunity to delineate their roles as community members. It has been received with great enthusiasm and has fostered both teacher and student participation in meaningful activities that directly benefit the community in which they live.

Community Service

To publish books and donate them to a local nursery school. Sample Evidence: The books.

To make better use of community resources. Sample Evidence: A student- and teacher-designed *Guide to Our Community.*

To continue my role as coordinator of a program which provides free home-cooked meals to shut-ins and to involve students in this program. Sample Evidence: Reflective entries from my journal.

Early Intervention

To offer support to first grade "at-risk" students and their families. Sample Evidence: Reading support materials, videotapes, meetings with parents.

Global Problems, Local Connections

Create an awareness of the problem of hunger in our world. Sample Evidence: Hunger awareness posters created by students, participation in community program to provide meals.

Parental Involvement

To actively involve parents in their child's education by using parent volunteers as guest speakers, readers, etc. Sample Evidence: Photographs, project posters.

To involve parents in helping students with social service projects to enhance the community. Sample Evidence: Photographs, videotapes.

To provide appropriate books for student independent reading at home. Sample Evidence: Handouts from parent workshop acquainting them with various genres and titles intended for developing readers.

To increase parental involvement in school activities. Sample Evidence: Parent meetings, photos, agendas.

To increase parents' awareness of a child's developmental writing process. Sample Evidence: Workshop to include parents in writing activities modeled at school which can be completed at home.

To teach a "Family Math" class to parents and students. Sample Evidence: Reflective journal entries of parents, students, and teacher.

To encourage parents to become an active participant in their child's education. Sample Evidence: Parent newsletter.

To share knowledge regarding inclusionary practices. Sample Evidence: Parent workshops, newsletter.

Increase parents understanding and use of technology to help their children and themselves. To work with the parent center to arrange for computers with appropriate child and adult software to be lent to parents. Sample Evidence: Copies of grants written to provide computer instruction and hardware, parent and student reactions.

Portfolio Assessment To share portfolio assessment information with parents. Sample Evidence: Parent workshop, reactions.

Senior Citizens To encourage the students to understand the needs of the elderly. Sample Evidence: Photographs of visits with seniors, "Adopt a Grandparent" program.

Senior Volunteers To encourage more senior citizens to volunteer in the school. Sample Evidence: Notes from a presentation to R.S.V.P.

School and Community Improvement To develop with students a plan to improve our school and community. Sample Evidence: The plan, improvements made.

Student Mentors To create a mentoring program for elementary school children with high school students to meet one evening a week at school. Sample Evidence: Evening tutoring sessions, student reactions.

Teach at Local University To teach a university course on young adult literature for the first time. Sample Evidence: Syllabus, videotape, student portfolio entries.

CONCLUSION: IMPLICATIONS FOR THE PORTFOLIO CULTURE

The Collaborative Model extends teacher assessment and evaluation from the traditional black and white snapshot of performance to an ongoing, full-color videotape. Its benefits are clear, and its implications for education as a profession are diverse. First, educators, teachers and administrators alike, view themselves as active participants in a community of learners. There are many indicators of this, including the fact that several administrators adapted the Collaborative Model to construct their own portfolios, which, in turn, have become the subjects of portfolio conversations. Second, the dynamic nature of the portfolios affords each participant the opportunity to offer direction to both the assessment and evaluation aspects of the process, as well as to his or her own professional development. Third, the type of assessment being used in the classroom is now being modeled by teachers and administrators within the district. This affirms that all involved value the process. Finally, the Collaborative Model of Teacher Evaluation incorporates each of the elements that Athanases (1994) suggested would most likely enhance teacher portfolios: relevant instructional emphases, reflection, and opportunities for personal discovery in interaction with other professionals.

Kieffer (1994) and his colleagues spoke about the potential of portfolios from parents' documentation of children's emergence into literacy to remembering a person's life-long contributions to society. The Collaborative Model fits somewhere in between these two purposes, but does indeed make its contribution to the portfolio culture. As one teacher has observed, "The Collaborative Model empowers teachers to become active participants in their own evaluations. Teachers determine the direction of the assessment. It also demands increased accountability. This model could revolutionize the process of teaching as we know it."

APPENDIXES

A. Portfolio Planner

B. Standards for Evaluation

C. Portfolio Rubrics for Individual Goals

D. Portfolio Rubrics for Completed Portfolios

E. Questions and Answers

- Collective Bargaining Agreements
- Professional Development
- Time Factors
- Weighting Goals
- Teacher Performance
- Role of Observation
- Reliability and Validity

APPENDIX A: PORTFOLIO PLANNER

The Portfolio Planner is used to assist teachers in thinking through the process of creating personal goals and aligning them with meaningful supporting performances. Because there are five categories within the Collaborative Model, separate Portfolio Planners are usually developed for each.* It is important to remember that there is no set number of evidences, so the length of the Portfolio Planner varies by goal.

Collaborative Model Portfolio Planner
Individual Category

Category One: Educational Philosophy

Name _____ District _____

School _____ Portfolio from _____ to _____

- Please list your proposed evidences in the spaces provided. Use additional sheets if necessary.
- In your rationale statement, briefly explain how your evidence relates to the goal.
- Remember to share copies of your Portfolio Planner for each goal with all team members at least two weeks prior to your team meeting.

Goal:_____

_____

_____

Portfolio Possibilities:

1. _____

Rationale: _____

_____

2. _____

Rationale: _____

_____

(Adapted from McLauglin & Vogt, 1996)

---

*Appendix A includes a sample Portfolio Planner for Category One: Educational Philosophy.

APPENDIX B: STANDARDS FOR EVALUATION

The Collaborative Model Standards for Evaluation are presented in Appendix B. These performance criteria serve as the foundation of portfolio evaluation. The standards are thoroughly delineated and may be used as presented. However, it is important to note that individual districts are encouraged to use the Standards as a foundation for collaboratively defining evaluative descriptors according to their respective contexts.

Collaborative Model
Standards for Evaluation

4.0 Exceptional application and depth of self-reflection are demonstrated. Initiative, creativity, independence, diversity, and risk-taking are evident. Performances are totally professional in appearance and are congruent with portfolio goals.

3.0 Thorough application and depth of self-reflection are demonstrated. Performances are diverse. Performances are very professional in appearance and are congruent with portfolio goals.

2.0 Adequate application and depth of self-reflection are demonstrated. Performances are somewhat diverse. Performances are professional in appearance and are mostly congruent with portfolio goals.

1.0 Inadequate application and depth of self-reflection are demonstrated. There is little variety in performances. Performances are less than professional in appearance and are minimally congruent with portfolio goals.

APPENDIX C: RUBRICS FOR INDIVIDUAL GOALS

A rubric for each individual goal is completed by the teacher as well as each team member. This information serves as the foundation for the completed portfolio rubric. It also facilitates the portfolio process because individual category goals can be completed at the teacher's convenience. Appendix C includes both Self-Evaluation and Team Member Evaluation Rubrics for an Individual Portfolio Goal.

Collaborative Model Rubric
Individual Portfolio Goal

Self-Evaluation

Name _____ District _____

School _____ Portfolio from ____ to ____

Goal: _____

- On the continuum please indicate the progress made toward attaining this goal.
- Write your reflection in the space provided. Use additional sheets if necessary.

Continuum:

Inadequate	Adequate	Thorough	Exceptional

◄─────────────────────────────►

Self-Reflection:

Teacher's Signature _____
Date _____

Collaborative Model Rubric
Individual Portfolio Goal
Team Member Evaluation

Teacher's Name _____ District _____

School _____ Portfolio from ____ to ____

Goal: _____

- On the continuum please indicate the progress made toward attaining this goal.

- Write your reflection in the space provided. Use additional sheets if necessary.

Continuum:

Inadequate   **Adequate**   **Thorough**   **Exceptional**

Reflection:

Team Member Signature _____
Date _____

APPENDIX D: RUBRICS FOR COMPLETED PORTFOLIO

Completed portfolios are evaluated by the entire team. Appendix D includes both Self-Evaluation and Team Member Evaluation Rubrics on which to record completed portfolio evaluations.

Collaborative Model Rubric
Completed Portfolio
Self-Evaluation

Teacher's Name _____ District _____

School _____ Portfolio from _____ to _____

- On the continuum please indicate the progress you believe your portfolio reflects.
- Write your self-reflection in the space provided. Use additional sheets if necessary.

Continuum:

Inadequate   Adequate   Thorough   Exceptional

⟵————————————————————————⟶

Self-Reflection:

Teacher's Signature_____
Date_____

Collaborative Model Rubric
Completed Portfolio
Team Member Evaluation

Teacher's Name _____ District _____

School _____ Portfolio from _____ to _____

Team Member: _____

- On the continuum, please show the progress you believe this portfolio reflects.
- Write your reflection in the space provided. Use additional sheets if necessary.

Continuum:

| Inadequate | Adequate | Thorough | Exceptional |

Reflection:

Team Member Signature_____

Date_____

APPENDIX E: QUESTIONS AND ANSWERS

1. How does the Collaborative Model interact with Collective Bargaining Agreements?

This is an issue that needs to be addressed by each district before the Collaborative Model is implemented. Because many Collective Bargaining Agreements already provide for professional growth plans for teachers, unions are generally open to discussions about some type of portfolio being part of the process. When the Model is introduced, there is usually interest and support for this type of multifaceted, performance-based assessment. Implementing the Collaborative Model also affords the union the opportunity to be seen in a progressive light for aligning teacher evaluation with innovative student assessment practices.

There is no doubt that the amount of work and time involved in the Collaborative Model is more demanding than the "observation only" teacher evaluation method. These issues need to be discussed openly. Once these concerns are addressed, the performance portfolio process is generally integrated with ease.

2. What kind of training do participants need to effectively use the Collaborative Model?

As with portfolio assessment in K–12 classrooms, training is essential for everyone involved in the process. An in-depth understanding of the portfolio process is integral to successful implementation and continued use of the Collaborative Model. Such training usually includes theory, application, sharing, and reflection.

Exploring the theoretical underpinnings of the portfolio process enables participants to understand the relationship between innovative assessment practices and current research. Practical application affords team members an opportunity to put theory into practice. At workshop sessions, participants typically generate ideas for personal use of the Collaborative Model. These experiences serve as the basis for sharing and, ultimately, reflecting. Sharing ideas reduces the ambiguity and reflection promotes ownership of the process.

Openness, collegiality, risk-taking, and respect for others are characteristics of not only successful training sessions, but also of the portfolio process as a whole. Training sessions may be tailored to each district's needs.

3. How do we explain to our peers that the benefits and rewards of the Collaborative Model far outweigh the time required to implement the Model?

When developing the Collaborative Model, consideration was given to time requirements. For this reason, the design is flexible, offering considerable latitude to participants. For example, portfolios may be structured over a two-year period, the number of goals and evidences may vary, and portfolio conversations may be scheduled as needed. Additional accommodations can be made for teachers experiencing particular difficulty.

There is no question that the Collaborative Model is more time-consuming than more traditional observations; however, in the portfolio process, time invested by teachers directly impacts teaching performance and student achievement. Most teachers have dealt successfully with the time issues by developing and maintaining their portfolios at the convenience of their personal schedules.

4. In our district, we see value in weighting the goals. How does this impact the effectiveness of the Model?

Because the Model is inherently flexible and is designed to accommodate the needs of individual districts, weighting the goals is a viable option. For example, for beginning teachers, a district may choose to weigh Curriculum and Instruction more heavily than Contributions to School and Community. Since the teachers' portfolio goals reflect long-term district goals, such accommodations are often part of the Collaborative Model's use.

5. Does a teacher ever submit an unsatisfactory portfolio?

The amount of support provided throughout the Collaborative Model reduces the possibility of an unsatisfactory rating. The Portfolio Planner, portfolio conversations, e-mail communications, and mentoring offer multiple opportunities for monitoring the process. In addition, the teacher-designed goals, multiple evidences, and input from various team members offer a very comprehensive view of teaching performance. Despite these precautions, it is still possible to create an unsatisfactory portfolio.

There is also the possibility of attaining an unsatisfactory rating within individual components of the Model. Because the portfolio process is multidimensional rather than unidimensional, as with observation alone, differences between effective and ineffective teachers are accentuated when the

Collaborative Model is utilized. For example, a highly effective teacher may include well-designed lesson plans and units that are supported by videotapes of demonstration lessons written by peers and/or supervisors and classroom portfolio data verifying student progress and learning. The ineffective teacher, on the other hand, while submitting well-designed lesson plans, may lack the additional supportive evidence to document effective teaching. Without such evidence, documentation would not be substantive enough to meet the standards set by the Collaborative Model.

6.   What role does observation play in the Collaborative Model?

Observation offers information about teaching performance that may be difficult to capture in any other way. For this reason, observations are generally included among the multiple evidences used to support a particular goal. It is, however, important to remember that in such observations "the teacher is viewed as an active constructor and possessor of knowledge—a problem solver . . . and the observer is a true observer, taking into account the context . . . posing collegial questions, and provoking the teacher to reflect on his/her performance" (Airasian, 1993, p. 62).

7.   What about issues of reliability and validity?

Reliability and validity are critical factors in all evaluation procedures. Gellman (1992, p.41) recommended that portfolios be "prepared to respond to a standard task or set of tasks" in order to promote reliability. The portfolio process used in the Collaborative Model meets this criterion. Although each portfolio reflects the individuality of its creator, a common set of criteria guide preparation. The teacher-created goals and portfolio possibilities contribute to uniformity and consistency. In addition, the Portfolio Planners, mentoring, portfolio conversations, sharing, collegial nature of the Model, and evaluation forms are all included to reduce ambiguity (McLaughlin & Vogt, 1996).

Concerning validity, Barton and Collins (1993) stated that portfolios represent a valid measure of student growth because they provide access to complex variables which contribute to overall learning and ability. The Collaborative Model validly measures teacher performance because it is "grounded in real work rather than artificial measures" (Stowell & Tierney, 1995, p. 81). Through the Model, teachers create and submit multiple, multidimensional indicators for each personal goal, offering a broader and deeper perception of teaching performance.

REFERENCES 🌰🌰⌒

Acker, S. (1995). Gender and teachers' work. In M.W. Apple (Ed.), *Review of Educational Research in Education, 21,* 99–162.

Airasian, P.W. (1993). Teacher assessment: Some issues for principals. *National Association of Secondary Principals Bulletin, 77*(555), 55–56.

Anderson, R.C., & Pearson, P.D. (1984). A schema-theoretic view of basic processes in reading comprehension. In P.D. Pearson (Ed.), *Handbook of reading research.* New York: Longman.

Association for Supervision and Curriculum Development. (1995). Looking for excellent teaching. *Education Update, 37*(3), 1–2.

Athanases, S.Z. (1994). Teachers' reports of the effects of preparing portfolios of literary instruction. *The Elementary School Journal, 94*(4), 421–439.

Baratz-Snowden, J. (1993). Assessment of teachers: A view from the national board for professional teaching standards. *Theory into Practice, 32*(2), 82–85.

Barth, R.S. (1993). Reflections on a conversation. *Journal of Personnel Evaluation in Education, 7,* 217–221.

Barton, J., & Collins, A. (1993). Portfolios in teacher education. *Journal of Teacher Education, 44*(3), 200–209.

Black, S. (1993). How teachers are reshaping evaluation procedures. *Educational Leadership, 51*(2), 38–42.

Blake, J., Bachman, J., Frys, M.K., Holbert, P., Ivan, T., & Sellitto, P. (1995). A portfolio-based assessment model for teachers: Encouraging professional growth. *National Association of Secondary School Principals Bulletin, 79*(573), 37–46.

Bryant, M., & Currin, D. (1995). Views of teacher evaluation from novice and expert evaluations. *Journal of Curriculum and Supervision, 10*(3), 250–261.

Cambourne, B., & Turnbill, J. (1988). *Coping with chaos.* Portsmouth, NH: Heinemann.

Carnegie Forum on Education and the Economy: Task Force on Teaching as a Profession. (1986). *A nation prepared: Teachers for the 21st Century.* Washington, DC: Author.

Chase, A., & Wolfe, P. (1989). Off to a good start in peer coaching. *Educational Leadership, 46*(8), 37–38.

Chrisco, I.M. (1989). Peer assistance works. *Educational Leadership, 46*(8), 31–34.

Colton, A., Sparks-Langer, G.M., Tripp-Opple, K., & Simmons, J.M. (1989). Collaborative inquiry into developing reflective pedagogical thinking. *Action in Teacher Education, XI*(3), 44–52.

Dagley, D.L., & Orso, J.K. (1991). Integrating summative, formative modes of evaluation. *National Association of Secondary Principals Bulletin, 75*(536), 72–82.

Daniels, H. (1994). *Literature circles: Voice and choice in the student centered classroom.* Maine: Stenhouse Publishers.

Darling-Hammond, L. (1996). The quiet revolution: Rethinking teacher development. *Educational Leadership, 53*(6), 4–10.

Dewey, J. (1904). *The relation of theory to practice in education.* The Third National Society of Education Yearbook (Part I). Chicago: University of Chicago Press.

Dewey, J. (1933). *How we think: A restatement of the relation of reflective thinking to the educative process.* Lexington, MA: D.C. Heath and Company.

Forman, E.A., & Cazden, C.B. (1994). Exploring Vygotskian perspectives in education: The cognitive value of peer interaction. In R. Ruddell, M.R. Ruddell, & H. Singer, (Eds.) *Theoretical models and processes of reading* (Fourth Edition). Newark, DE: International Reading Association.

Gambrell, L., & Almasi, J. (Eds.). (1996). *Lively Discussions creating classroom cultures that foster discussion, interpretation, and comprehension of text.* Newark, DE: International Reading Association.

Glickman, C.D., & Bey, T.M. (1990). Supervision. In W.R. Houston (Ed.), *Handbook of research on teacher education.* New York: Macmillan.

Goldhammer, R., Anderson, R.H., & Krajewski, R.J. (1980). *Clinical supervision: Special methods for the supervision of teachers* (2nd ed.). New York: Holt, Rinehart, and Winston.

Haefele, D.L. (1993). Evaluating teachers: A call for change. *Journal of Personnel Evaluation in Education, 7,* 21–31.

Hardcastle, B. (1988). Spiritual connections: Proteges' reflections on significant mentorships. *Theory into Practice, 27*(3), 201–208.

Hiebert, E.H., Valencia, S.W., & Afflerbach, P.P. (1994). *Authentic reading assessment: Practices and possibilities.* Newark, DE: International Reading Association.

Hirsch, S., & Ponder, G. (1991). New plots, new heroes in staff development. *Educational Leadership, 49*(3), 43–48.

Hollingsworth, S. (1992). Learning to teach through collaborative conversation: A feminist approach. *American Educational Research Journal, 29,* 373–404.

Holmes Group (1986). *Tomorrow's teachers: A report of the Holmes Group.* East Lansing, MI: Author.

Holmes Group (1990). *Tomorrow's schools: Principles for the design of professional development schools.* East Lansing, MI: Author.

Kieffer, R.D. (1994, December). Portfolio process and teacher change. *National Reading Research Center News, 8.* Publication Draft.

Killion, J., & Todnem, G. (1991). A process for personal theory building. *Educational Leadership, 48*(6), 14–16.

Levine, S.L. (1993). Developmental assessment: Accounting for adult growth in supervision and evaluation. *Journal of Personnel Evaluation in Education, 7,* 223–230.

Lomask, M.S., Pecheone, R.L., & Boykoff-Baron, J. (1995). Assessing new science teachers. *Educational Leadership, 52*(6), 62–65.

Marczely, B. (1992). Teacher evaluation: Research versus practice. *Journal of Personnel Evaluation in Education, 5,* 279–290.

McLaughlin, M. (1995). *Performance assessment: A practical guide to implementation.* Boston: Houghton Mifflin.

McLaughlin, M., & Kennedy, A. (1993). *Pennsylvania's Chapter V revisions: An administrator's guide.* Princeton, NJ: Houghton Mifflin.

McLaughlin, M., & Vogt, M.E. (1995). *Performance portfolios for inservice teachers: A collaborative model.* Paper presented at the 45th Annual Meeting of the National Reading Conference, New Orleans, LA.

McLaughlin, M., & Vogt, M.E. (1996). *Portfolios in teacher education.* Newark, DE: International Reading Association.

National Board for Professional Teaching Standards. (1989). *Toward high and rigorous standards for the teaching profession.* Washington, DC: Author.

National Commission on Excellence in Education. (1983). *A nation at risk: The imperative for educational reform.*

Odell, S.J. (1990). Support for new teachers. In T. Bey & C.T. Holmes (Eds.), *Mentoring: Developing successful new teachers.* Reston, VA: Association of Teacher Educators.

Olivero, J.L., & Heck, J. (1994). Staff Evaluation: Putting the pieces together for a strategic advantage. *National Association of Secondary School Principals Bulletin, 78*(565), 60–68.

Paris, S. (1991). Portfolio assessment for young readers. *The Reading Teacher, 44,* 680–681.

Pearson, P.D. (1985). Changing the face of reading comprehension instruction. *The Reading Teacher, 38,* 724–738.

Pikulski, J.J. (1990). The role of tests in a literacy assessment program. *The Reading Teacher, 43,* 686–688.

Poole, W. (1995). Reconstructing the teacher-administrator relationship to achieve systemic change. *Journal of School Leadership, 5,* 565–596.

Raney, P., & Robbins, P. (1989). Professional growth and support through peer coaching. *Educational Leadership, 46*(8), 35–39.

Reagan, T., Case, K., Case, C.W., & Freiberg, J.A. (1993). Reflecting on "reflective practice": Implications for teacher evaluation. *Journal of Personnel Evaluation in Education, 6,* 263–277.

Regan, H.B. (1993). Integrated portfolios as tools for differentiated teacher evaluation: A proposal. *Journal of Personnel Evaluation in Education, 7,* 275–290.

Ruddell, M.R. (1996). *Teaching Content Reading and Writing* (2nd Edition). Boston: Allyn & Bacon.

Schon, D. (1987). *Educating the reflective practitioner.* San Francisco: Jossey-Bass.

Setteducati, D. (1995). Portfolio self-assessment for teachers: A reflection on the Farmingdale. *Journal of Staff Development, 16*(3), 2–5.

Shepard, L. (1989). Why we need better assessments. *Educational Leadership, 46*(7), 4–9.

Showers, B., & Joyce, B. (1996). The evolution of peer coaching. *Educational Leadership, 53*(6), 12–16.

Shulman, L.S. (1988). A union of insufficiencies: Strategies for teacher assessment in a period of reform. *Educational Leadership, 46*(3), 36–39.

Sikorski, M.F., Niemiec, R.P., & Walberg, H.J. (1994). Best teaching practices: A checklist for observations. *National Association of Secondary School Principals Bulletin, 78*(561), 50–54.

Stewart, R.A. & Paradis, E.E. (1992). *Portfolios: Agents of change and empowerment in classrooms.* A paper presented at the 42nd Annual Meeting of the National Reading Conference, San Antonio, Texas.

Stowell, L.P., & Tierney, R.J. (1995). Portfolios in the classroom: What happens when teachers and students negotiate assessment? In R.L. Allington & S.A. Walmsley (Eds.), *No quick fix: Rethinking literacy programs in America's elementary schools* (pp. 78–94). New York: Teachers College Press; Newark, DE: International Reading Association.

Sweeney, J. (1994). New paradigms in teacher evaluation: The SBESD model. *Journal of Personnel Evaluation in Education, 8,* 223–237.

Tierney, R.J., Carter, M.A., & Desai, L.E. (1991). *Portfolio assessment in the reading-writing classroom.* Norwood, MA: Christopher-Gordon.

Tuckman, B.W. (1995). Assessing effective teaching. *Peabody Journal of Education, 70*(2), 127–138.

Valencia, S.(1990). A portfolio approach to classroom reading assessment: The whats, whys, and hows. *The Reading Teacher, 43,* 338–340.

Vann, A.S. (1996). An alternative assessment for master teachers. *Principal, 75*(3), 29–30.

Vartuli, S., & Fyfe, B. (1993). Teachers need developmentally appropriate practices too. *Young Children, 48*(4), 36–42.

Verga, M. (1997). *Literature circles.* Workshop presented at the Los Angeles County Goals 2000 K–3 Literacy Conference, Los Angeles, CA.

Vogt, M.E., McLaughlin, M., & Ruddell, M.R. (1993). *Do as I do: Using portfolios to evaluate students in reading methods courses.* Paper presented at the 43rd Annual Meeting of the National Reading Conference, Charleston, SC.

Vygotsky, L. (1978). *Mind in society.* Cambridge, MA: Harvard University Press.

Whalen, E., & DeRose, M. (1993). The power of peer appraisals. *Educational Leadership, 51*(2), 44–48.

Wink, J. (1997). *Critical pedagogy: Notes from the real world.* White Plains, NY: Longman Publishers.

Winograd, P., Paris, S., & Bridge, C. (1991). Improving the assessment of literacy. *The Reading Teacher, 45,* 108–116.

Wood, C.J. (1992). Toward more effective teacher evaluation: Lessons from naturalistic inquiry. *National Association of Secondary School Principals Bulletin, 76*(542), 52–59.

Worthen, B. (1993). Critical issues that will determine the future of alternative assessment. *Phi Delta Kappan, 74*(6), 444–454.

ABOUT THE AUTHORS

Maureen McLaughlin is a Professor of Education at East Sroudsburg State University of Pennsylvania. She earned her doctorate at Boston University in reading and language development. Prior to her tenure in the Pennsylvania State System of Higher Education, Dr. McLaughlin spent fifteen years as a classroom teacher, reading specialist, and department chair in a public school system.

Dr. McLaughlin is senior author of Houghton Mifflin's *Classroom Guide to Performance Assessment* and author of Houghton Mifflin's *Mathematics Performance Assessment: A Practical Guide to Implementation.* She is also co-author of the *International Reading Association's Portfolios in Teacher Education.*

In addition, Dr. McLaughlin is chair of the International Reading Association's Assessment Committee and chair of the National Reading Conference's Ethics Committee. She is a frequent speaker at international, national, and state conferences and is an educational consultant to school districts and universities nationwide.

Mary Ellen Vogt is an Associate Professor of Education at California State Universtiy, Long Beach, where she teaches courses in reading and language development. Prior to the University she served as a classroom teacher, special education teacher, reading specialist, and district resource teacher. She received her doctorate in Language and Literacy from the University of California, Berkeley. Dr. Vogt is past president of the California Reading Association and recently completed a three-year term on the Board of Directors of the International Reading Association. She has served on editorial advisory boards and published numerous articles and chapters. In addition, Dr. Vogt is a co-author of *Portfolios in Teacher Education* and an author of the 1997 reading series *Invitations to Literacy* published by Houghton Mifflin. In 1994, she received the Marcus Foster Memorial Award for Outstanding Contributions to the Field of Reading in California. In November 1997, she was inducted into the California Reading Hall of Fame.

Portfolio Presentations in Teacher Education: Rites of Passage for the Emerging Professional

Section II

Portfolio Presentations in Teacher Education: Rites of Passage for the Emerging Professional

Joanne Anderson
Judith Du Mez
Marian Graeven Peter

INTRODUCTION

As educational systems move away from the exclusive use of standardized tests as measures of professional competence, portfolios are gaining ground as effective tools that accurately reflect the learning processes of teacher candidates. Our purpose in writing this chapter is to share the journey we have taken as we move from old standards of evaluation toward more authentic assessment. We specifically chose the implementation of portfolio presentations as a process for screening and as a product for documenting the developing competencies of teacher candidates. After searching for appropriate resources and guidelines, we found the theoretical base but not the necessary practical support for implementing portfolio presentations. Therefore, we began anew in developing our own portfolio system.

Our particular Teacher Education Program offers certification in early childhood; early childhood exceptional education needs; and elementary, middle, and secondary education with various majors and minors in the liberal arts. Enrollment in the program is in excess of 600 students. Because we strive to ensure that our graduates will be educators who are caring, effective decision makers, *The Teacher as Reflective Decision Maker* is the theme for the program. Based upon the beliefs of the faculty, the Division Mission Statement, and the Mission of the College, a professional knowledge base was designed to support and carry out the theme. Derived from research, theory, and practice, the professional knowledge base is organized around seven categories: expectations, management, motivation, instruction, modeling, individualization/grouping, and assessment (Good & Brophy, 1994). The faculty of the Teacher Education Program is committed to remain current in the professional knowledge base and to teach and model strategies that will enable the candidates to enter the field ready and able to assume the role of beginning teacher. As teacher candidates move through the certification program, they are expected to demonstrate competency in each of these seven categories of the knowledge base.

Intellectually we understand that educational systems need to focus on the *demonstration* of developing competencies that tie directly to the professional skills and performance indicators of each particular certification program. Research findings confirm that the overall assessment of teacher education students by means of standardized tests and grade point averages (GPAs) are not necessarily the best indicators of competencies in the professional field (Touzel, 1993). We began our work by looking at various means of authentic assessment that would: (a) involve higher-level thinking while producing individualized performance-based products, (b) incorporate assessment tasks that teach, and (c) require judgments that are routinely found in the real world that test professional knowledge.

The portfolio is one type of authentic assessment that is often mentioned in the literature. The use of portfolios is emerging as one of the major trends in education in the United States, in both higher education and K–12 school systems. Portfolios are more than just a container full of "stuff." A portfolio is a structured collection documenting a person's progress, achievements, and contributions that are both selective and reflective. For our purposes, portfolios are authentic, learner-specific documents, which when reviewed against criteria for evaluation, give evidence of growth and development toward becoming teachers.

Using this theoretical framework, we designed an assessment process that accurately reflects the learning of our teacher candidates. The portfolio process not only has increased our students' understanding of the program's knowledge base, but also has allowed us to build in time for mutual reflec-

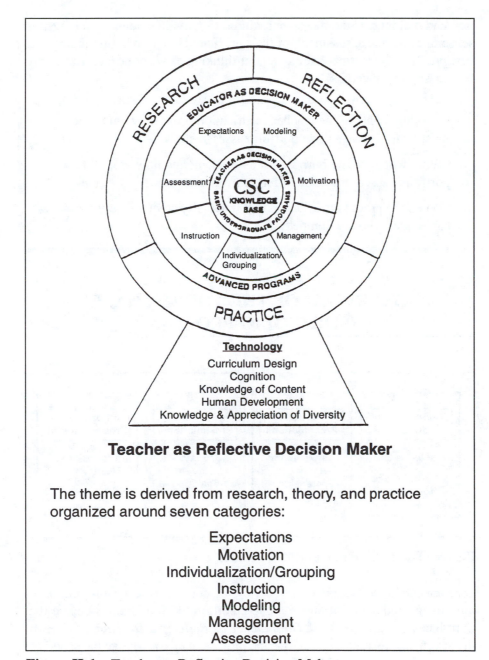

Teacher as Reflective Decision Maker

The theme is derived from research, theory, and practice organized around seven categories:

Expectations
Motivation
Individualization/Grouping
Instruction
Modeling
Management
Assessment

Figure II-1   Teacher as Reflective Decision Maker

tion and dialogue. Candidates are required to provide evidence, in the truest sense of authentic assessment, of their proficiency in translating theory into best practice. Questions that guided our thinking as we conceptualized portfolio assessment were:

"At what points in the teacher certification program would it be most beneficial to utilize portfolio assessment?"

"What would be the purpose for assessment and how would the portfolio presentations be different from each other?"

"When the process is in place, will it actually advance <u>only</u> those candidates who are competent?"

OVERVIEW OF THE THREE-PHASE PORTFOLIO PROCESS

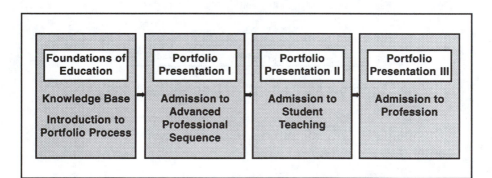

Figure II-2 Three-Phase Portfolio Process

Teacher candidates receive an overview of our certification program's requirements and expectations in a one-credit, initial foundations course that introduces: (a) the theme of *The Teacher as Reflective Decision Maker,* (b) the seven categories that comprise the professional knowledge base, and (c) the portfolio process. Although each phase of the portfolio process will be described in detail, a brief synopsis follows:

Portfolio Presentation I: As a rite of passage into advanced professional course work, teacher candidates are required to compile and present a portfolio that contains carefully selected artifacts representing the categories of the knowledge base. In addition, a writing sample that reflects the student's understanding of educational and political current issues is evaluated. Information gathered from faculty questionnaires regarding personal dispositions is critiqued by each teacher candidate during a facilitated conversation.

Portfolio Presentation II: Following the professional course work, Portfolio Presentation II serves as the candidate's admission to student teaching. It is at this time that the original portfolio, refined and enhanced, gives evidence of meeting the necessary competencies to allow the candidate to student teach. Personal interviews play a critical role in this presentation.

Portfolio Presentation III: After successfully completing student teaching, Portfolio Presentation III is the teacher candidate's admission to the teaching profession. The portfolio now becomes a marketing tool that enables students to give evidence of their expertise to members of the broader educational community. Although this presentation is viewed as a culminating activity of the student's formal preparation, it is also a time to celebrate the beginning of one's career as a teacher.

PORTFOLIO PRESENTATION I

When first discussing the possibility of portfolios, students brought forth concerns, questions, and comments.

> "This wasn't in my original requirements; it just sounds like busy work!"
>
> "Who's bright idea is this?"
>
> "We've discussed portfolio assessment in our classes; now we'll get to see it first-hand."
>
> "What is this portfolio supposed to look like? Do we get a model to follow?"
>
> "I haven't kept any of my work. What am I supposed to put in this portfolio?"

GRAPHIC ORGANIZER FOR
PORTFOLIO PRESENTATION I

Rationale
Methodology
Introduction to the Initial Certification Program
Student Orientation Sessions
    Requirements
    Application
    Calendar
    Office Portfolio
    Portfolio Organization Guidelines
    Outcomes/Assessment/Criteria
    Disposition and Attitude Questionnaires
    Appeal Process
    Agenda
Faculty Facilitator Orientation Session
The Portfolio Presentation I Session
    Current Issue
    Presentation of the Portfolio
    Disposition and Attitude Questionnaires
    Student Evaluation of Portfolio Presentation I
Assessment by the Facilitators
Final Report and Recommendation

RATIONALE

As teacher candidates reach the end of their sophomore year, they must participate in, and successfully pass, a screening process known as Portfolio Presentation I. In essence, this allows the students to be admitted to the professional sequence and take the advanced curriculum and methods courses. In the past, we used an in-house assessment process which took the form of a seminar. Teacher candidates were placed in small cohort groups and questioned by a faculty facilitator as to why they had chosen education as their profession. This seminar was not connected in any way to our knowledge base, and a candidate's success relied mainly on grade point averages and scores from standardized tests. The old process did not assess the dispositions of the candidates nor did the process require them to reflect upon and document their developing competencies. A major concern of the faculty was that the reputation of the college certification program might be diminished in the community because a handful of students had passed through an obsolete screening mechanism.

As program developers, we recognized the tremendous potential of implementing a portfolio process. At the same time we had a variety of questions and concerns.

"Wherever will we find the time to do this?"

"Will this new portfolio process draw focus to our program or further fragment it?"

"Is this really going to benefit students in the job market?"

"Will members of the educational community support our efforts by requiring portfolios as part of the interview process?"

METHODOLOGY

When we began to develop the process for implementing portfolios, we found some helpful information on methodology in *Fastback 379: Portfolio Development for Preservice Teachers* (Nettles & Petrick, 1995). The authors used a six-step methodology in initiating the portfolio process; we adopted and modified the methodology to suit the needs of our certification program.

Step 1. Adopt a philosophy statement—The effective implementation of a portfolio begins with discussions on philosophy. It is important to reach consensus about the learning theories that guide and shape the particular teacher education program. After consensus on the philosophy is reached, a single, succinct statement should be developed that focuses thinking and guides the creation of the portfolio.

Teachers must make decisions based on knowledge of content and best practices. Therefore, at our institution, as part of a two-year-long strategic planning process for the Teacher Education Division, we adopted the philosophy statement of *The Teacher as Reflective Decision Maker.*

Step 2. Decide on outcomes that reflect the teacher education program—Outcomes, or performance indicators, are specific behaviors that are deemed necessary for good teaching to occur. The use of outcomes is vital; they are the statements that guide the building of the portfolio and the goals that teacher candidates must achieve. Outcomes need to be comprehensive and reflect the faculty's belief in what it is teachers should know and be able to do.

At our institution, we used the seven areas of the professional knowledge base as the outcomes that reflect our program. During each of the successive portfolio presentations, teacher candidates are expected to document growth in the understanding and application of each area. The section on implementation will present this assessment.

Step 3. Determine the rationale for using portfolios—Portfolios used in preservice teacher education have several purposes. They can: (a) replace or supplement standardized testing and written examinations, (b) allow the teacher candidate to become familiar with alternative assessment so they can better visualize its use in K–12 classrooms, (c) promote dialogue and reflection about the process of teaching as teacher candidates discuss the personal and professional insights they have documented in their portfolios, and (d) provide higher-education faculty with opportunities to reflect upon the effectiveness of their program and to revise outcomes, courses, and assignments.

As the portfolio process developed, it became a celebration of learning and a rite of passage as students completed one phase and moved to another. The process validates the three major purposes of portfolios as: (a) a screening device that documents active student learning, (b) a marketing tool that enables students to present evidence of competency, and (c) a means of providing feedback to faculty regarding program effectiveness.

Step 4. Select specific types of artifacts the teacher candidate will include to document outcomes—An artifact is material evidence found in a portfolio that documents learning and developing competencies. Examples include lesson plans, videos, photographs, entries from reflective journals, and evaluations from supervisors. Ideas for artifacts can come from classroom assignments, work in the field, or can reflect the personal and professional life of the individual teacher candidate.

Our program's Portfolio Guidelines are given to students and contain suggestions for artifact inclusion that are tied to the professional knowledge base. Although we provide some ideas for the types of artifacts candidates may choose to include in their portfolio, we have given students a fairly wide berth in creating something that is individual and truly represents them.

Step 5.   Decide on a process for implementing portfolios—The process for implementation depends upon the purpose for using portfolios, as well as how and when the education department intends to measure student progress, change, or improvement. It is important to remember that building a portfolio is a process that leads to a product. A portfolio documents growth throughout the academic career of the teacher candidate.

We have chosen a three-phase portfolio presentation process. The first two presentations either facilitate a student proceeding in the program or draw attention to concerns about the student's (a) academic work, (b) understanding of the knowledge base, (c) oral and written communication skills, and (d) attitudes and behaviors (dispositions). The third presentation provides the candidate with an opportunity to share his or her professional portfolio with members of the educational community who are prospective employers.

Step 6. Write guidelines for faculty and teacher candidates—Guidelines promote understanding of the portfolio process and can be made available as handouts during orientation sessions for teacher candidates and training sessions for facilitators. The written materials used during our portfolio presentations are included in this book as each phase is presented.

INTRODUCTION TO THE INITIAL CERTIFICATION PROGRAM

The easiest way for the reader to understand this portfolio process is to view the teacher certification program sequentially. The foundations are laid in the introductory course which is a requirement for every student. The course gives candidates an overview of the program and its requirements:

- Various certifications offered at Cardinal Stritch College,
- Grade point average (GPA) criteria,
- English Proficiency Requirement Test (EPRT); passing this college-based test in reading and writing is part of the requirements for graduation,
- Praxis 1/Pre-professional Skills Test (PPST); a state-mandated standardized test in math, reading, and writing that must be passed in its entirety before student teaching,
- The professional knowledge base and the seven categories that it comprises,

- Portfolio construction that is tied to the knowledge base,
- The portfolio presentation process,
- Clinical experiences in the field,
- The importance of appropriate attitudes and dispositions, and
- Commitment to the profession.

All the information regarding the initial certification program is delineated in the Teacher Education Handbook which each student receives in this introductory course. In addition to the overview of program sequence and requirements, students discuss and reflect upon issues currently affecting educational practice. Candidates write reviews on three of these issues and make a commitment, in the form of a contract, to track one issue throughout their program. The issues they select become the basis for a writing sample that is assessed during Portfolio Presentation I.

CURRENT EDUCATIONAL ISSUE
SAMPLE CONTRACT

The current educational issue I have chosen to follow throughout my studies at Cardinal Stritch College is:

_____

                          _____

                                  Signed

                          _____

                                  Date

Oral and written proficiency is stressed and assessed in the introductory course as a necessity for teacher candidates. At the end of the course, conferences are held with students regarding their prognosis for success in the program. They are assigned an education advisor who meets with them each semester to help select classes, remind them of program requirements, and answer questions. When candidates approach the end of their sophomore year and have completed the required preprofessional education classes, they are advised to apply for Portfolio Presentation I and to attend an orientation session. The students brought forth a variety of questions at the orientation session.

"Are you going to tell us exactly what we need to put in our portfolio?"

"Will faculty be willing to review our portfolio before the presentations?"

"When is everything due?"

"Do I have to show every part of my portfolio during my presentation?"

"Can I check on what current issue I said I'd track?"

"What's a disposition questionnaire?"

"Are we graded on this?"

"What happens if I don't pass?"

"What's going to happen the evening of the presentations?"

"Instead of a hard copy, can we put our portfolio on a computer diskette?"

STUDENT ORIENTATION SESSIONS

After the dates for the Portfolio I orientation sessions are established by members of the Teacher Education Program, they are listed in the education calendar and posted for student reference. Several orientation sessions are given, and the orientation is videotaped for students who cannot attend one of the scheduled meetings. Each session lasts an hour and a half. Orientations are generally held within the first two weeks in the semester; the portfolios are presented one month later. Teacher candidates receive application materials and guidelines for portfolio development during the orientation session. The remainder of this section will briefly describe each of these.

Requirements

Each orientation session begins with an overview of the portfolio process and the steps in the sequence of the certification program. Students are reminded of prerequisites that must have been fulfilled in order to apply for Portfolio Presentation I. These requirements are reviewed during the orientation session and are presented to the teacher candidates in writing. If the candidates do not meet the criteria, they may not apply to participate in Portfolio Presentation I until all requirements have been met. In addition, students are reminded that this presentation is a rite of passage, and they are expected to dress and act as a professional.

Portfolio Presentation I
Requirements

Applicant must:

- Complete Ed/Sed 100 or 101 Introduction to Education
- Complete Ed/SEd 200 Initial General Clinical Experience and Human Relations
- Earn an overall grade point average of 2.75
- Receive a minimum grade of B- in Communication Arts 101, English 101, English 102
- Pass two out of the three portions of the PPST
- Pass the English proficiency requirement test
- Prepare a portfolio for submission

All eligible students MUST attend the Portfolio Presentation Orientation meetings. These dates will be posted and listed in the Teacher Education Calendar. There are NO EXCEPTIONS to attending the orientation meetings.

Application

If requirements have been met, an application form is completed by the teacher candidate. This application is used for expediency to ensure the eligibility of the student and to designate the three faculty members that the student has asked to complete disposition questionnaires.

Portfolio Presentation I
Application

Name _____ Student ID Number _____

Address _____

Phone Number _____

Certification Area: Major _____ Certifiable Minor _____

(if applicable)

Status: Traditional _____ PBC _____

Clinical Status (Check one):

I have completed Ed/SEd 200 ____

I am presently enrolled in Ed/SEd 200 ____

I have successfully completed the English Proficiency Requirement Test (undergraduates only)

Grammar _____   Essay _____
Semester/Year   Semester/Year

I have successfully completed the Pre Professional Skills Test:

Reading: Score ____ Mathematics: Score ____ Writing: Score ____
Date _____   Date _____   Date _____

Names of faculty members asked to submit Disposition Questionnaires:

1. _____

2. _____

3. _____

The current educational issue I am tracking is:

_____

Dates for attendance at Portfolio Presentation I will be posted on the information board across from RLC 27.

Calendar

Students are given a calendar outlining the procedures for application and a timeline of the events in the Portfolio I process. Each critical due date is listed as a reminder for the students.

Portfolio Presentation I
Sample Calendar

August:	Semester begins
September 9–10:	Portfolio Orientation for students
September 27:	Dispositions due
October 10–11:	Portfolio Presentation I sessions
October 15:	Review Board meets
October 25:	Teacher Education Committee (TEC) meets
November:	Students with stipulations meet with faculty facilitators
December 15:	Stipulations due and stipulation forms sent to TEC

Office Portfolio

The office portfolio is a file maintained on each student by the education department. This portfolio contains information such as test scores, GPA, pertinent course work, evaluations from work in the field, service hours, and the student's current issue contract. The office portfolio is made available to the faculty facilitators at the time of Portfolio Presentation I to increase their understanding of the applicant.

Portfolio Presentation I
Office Portfolio

Name _____ Student ID Number _____

Date entered _____ Certification _____

Status: Undergraduate _____ PBC _____

PPST/Praxis I	Writing	Reading	Mathematics
Score	_____	_____	_____
Date Passed	_____	_____	_____

GPA   Overall _____   Education _____

Transcript for Portfolio Presentation I _____

Grades: En 101 _____   En 102_____   CA 101 _____

EPRT *undergrad only   Grammar: Date Passed _____
                        Essay: Date Passed _____

Writing Sample *Ed/SEd 100/101   No Concerns   Concerns
                                 _____   _____

Faculty Letter *Ed/SEd 100/101   Attended Conference ___
                                 Commendation ___ Concern ___

Disposition Surveys	Rec'd	No Concerns	Concerns
_____	____	1. _____	_____
_____	____	2. _____	_____
_____	____	3. _____	_____
<u>Ed/SEd 204/504</u> _____	____	4. _____	_____

Rubric: Ed/SEd 204/504   No Concerns __ Concerns ___

Clinical Evaluations for Ed/SEd 200   No Concerns __ Concerns ___

Current Issue: Ed/SEd 100/101: _____

Port I Facilitators' Recommendation: Pass __ Pass with Concerns __ Deny __
Port I TEC's Recommendation: Pass __ Pass with Concerns __ Deny __
                                       Date _____

Portfolio Organization Guidelines

Portfolio organization guidelines have been developed as a tool to help the student select appropriate artifacts to include in their portfolio. The essential understanding for the student is that the portfolio should represent their best work and should reflect the seven categories of the professional knowledge base. A narrative introduces the portfolio and provides the teacher candidate with an opportunity to share both personal and professional experiences. Because the multicultural/diverse learner perspective is a major focus of the initial certification program, it is important for the students to reflect a diversity perspective in their portfolios.

Although most students present their portfolios in a hard copy format using a binder or file system, some have begun to employ technology such as hyperstudio. We can see exciting possibilities on the horizon as students utilize more technological programs for organizing their portfolios. However, since some individuals in the marketplace may not have the technology or expertise to access materials presented in this manner, we continue to recommend that students have a hard copy of their portfolio available when interviewing.

Portfolio Presentation I
Portfolio Organization Guidelines

Portfolios will be organized according to the following criteria:

Introduction: Personal Narrative

Basic to all teacher preparation is exploring who you are and what you bring to your education and your future teaching. Your personality, philosophy, attitudes and belief systems impact on your teaching style, your students, and your colleagues.

a. **Required:** A personal narrative (Two pages maximum of written text.)

b. **Optional:** No more than three additional artifacts which could include: a resume, representative documentation from previous professions, representative documentation from general education courses, and/or something that depicts you and your personality.

Your portfolio must reflect a **multicultural/diverse learner perspective.** *To accomplish this, you may include any of the following:*

a. reflection of service hours

b. lesson plans/papers targeted to diverse populations

c. papers from multicultural class

d. clinical logs

e. additional appropriate material

Seven Specific Categories that Support the Professional Knowledge Base of Teacher as Decision Maker

Each of the following categories should contain 1 or 2 artifacts. The inclusion of each artifact must be accompanied by an explanation of what it is, what course it is from, and how it relates to the portfolio requirement. If the artifact reflects a multicultural/diverse learner perspective, highlight how it does so.

1. Expectations

Expectations are those standards teachers hold for students. Possible artifacts to include:

a. Unit outcomes

b. Lesson behavioral objectives/plans

c. Teacher Belief Inventory

d. Papers related to meeting student needs or setting expectations for students

e. Additional appropriate materials

2. Modeling

Modeling is showing students exactly how to perform a task and/or explicitly how to use a mental process. Modeling is implicit in how a teacher relates to students and others. Possible artifacts to include:

a. Papers on modeling as an effective strategy

b. Lesson plans with a strong modeling component

c. Appropriate artifacts from clinical observation logs

d. Careful description of how a teacher might model a particular skill, or process

e. Additional appropriate materials

3. Motivation

Motivational strategies are those strategies employed by teachers that cause the student to begin, continue, and complete assignments and activities in the classroom. Possible artifacts to include:

a. Papers on motivational strategies or the theory of motivation

b. Lesson plans with strong anticipatory sets or other motivational components

c. Description of motivational strategies used in lessons

d. Instructional tools or aids with a brief description of how they might motivate students

e. Additional appropriate materials

4. Management

Classroom management is a process of establishing and maintaining effective learning behaviors. Classroom management strategies are closely associated with and should be designed to support instruction. Possible artifacts to include:

a. Management plan

b. Papers on management strategies

c. Appropriate entries from a clinical observation log

d. Critique of management strategies

e. Additional appropriate materials

5. Individualization/Grouping

Individualization/grouping refers to accommodations that must be made to allow for differences in learning time and learning ability. Grouping is one way by which these differences are accommodated. Teachers employ strategies to accommodate diverse and individual student needs through a variety of classroom configurations. Possible artifacts to include:

a. Papers on grouping practices

b. Lesson plans with individualization/grouping strategies

c. Descriptions/critiques of different grouping strategies

d. IFSPs or IEPs

e. Additional appropriate materials

6. Instruction

Instruction refers to strategies employed by teachers in their interactions with students which enable the students to learn and succeed. Possible artifacts to include:

a. Lesson plans

b. Videotapes or audiotapes

c. Papers/descriptions of instructional strategies

d. Additional appropriate materials

7. Assessment

Assessment is a process of gathering multiple indicators of student performance in order to make effective instructional decisions. It is also the process of self-evaluation through which teachers investigate their own effectiveness. Possible artifacts to include:

a. Personal entries in reflective logs or journals where you are evaluating your effectiveness or the effectiveness of others

b. Self-assessments of clinical goals

c. Assessment plan

d. Critique of lesson plans and or videotapes

e. Additional appropriate materials

Optional Additional Data

This category is designed to incorporate all seven categories of the professional knowledge base of Teacher as Decision Maker. Possible artifacts to include:

anecdotal records of good practices
computer software with which you have familiarity
demonstration of computer expertise
literature logs
article summaries
bulletin board ideas
copies of awards
statement of your philosophy of discipline
lesson plans
reflective journals
units
observation reports
position papers
peer critiques
sample parent letters
clinical evaluations
videotapes

Outcomes/Assessment/Criteria

There are four separate components in Portfolio Presentation I. The students will be assessed according to specific criteria for each of these four areas:

1. Writing sample. The inclusion of the writing sample is necessitated by the importance of reviewing students' writing competencies and their ability to track and reflect upon their chosen educational issue.

2. Portfolio content. Portfolios are evaluated according to appropriateness of artifacts and rationale for inclusion.

3. Presentation of portfolio. Students must orally present their analysis of the portfolio and the implication it has on the remainder of their program.

4. Attitude and dispositions. Questionnaires from faculty are reviewed by the students and compared to the questionnaire they complete.

Portfolio Presentation I
Outcomes/Assessment/Criteria
Student Orientation

1. The student will be able to demonstrate in writing his/her understanding of a pre-chosen educational issue.

Criteria	Met	Not met at this time
a. Issue has been clearly defined.	_____	_____
b. Impact of issue on field of education and on the individual educator has been clearly stated.	_____	_____
c. Writing is well-organized, clear, and has minimal usage errors.	_____	_____

Comments:

Pass _____   **Low Pass** _____   **No Pass** _____
All met: Pass   Mixture: Low Pass   No criteria met: No Pass

2. The student will be able to demonstrate to the educational community his/her developing competency through the compilation of a professional portfolio.

Criteria	Met	Not met at this time
a. Portfolio meets or exceeds written student guidelines for appropriate artifacts in designated categories.	_____	_____
b. Each artifact has accompanying explanation for its inclusion.	_____	_____
c. A multicultural/diverse learner perspective is evident.	_____	_____
d. Portfolio contents display correct grammar, spelling, and punctuation.	_____	_____

Comments:

Pass _____   **Low Pass** _____   **No Pass** _____
All met: Pass   Mixture: Low Pass   No criteria met: No Pass

3. The student will be able to review the contents of his/her portfolio, express his/her analysis of the work, and set appropriate goals for his/her advanced professional sequence. (Presentation limited to 15 minutes.)

Criteria	*Met*	*Not met at this time*
a. Student identifies strengths of portfolio contents as they relate to becoming an effective teacher and reflective decision maker.	_____	_____
b. Student identifies areas of the portfolio contents where support and time are needed.	_____	_____
c. Student identifies follow-through on faculty feed-back to date.	_____	_____
d. Student identifies goals to pursue during course work in the advanced professional sequence.	_____	_____
e. Student presents self in a poised and polished manner.	_____	_____

Comments:

Pass _____   **Low Pass** _____   **No Pass** _____
All met: Pass   Mixture: Low Pass   No criteria met: No Pass

4. The student will be able to provide the educational community with information regarding the proximity of the match between the student's perception of his/her personal dispositions and the way the student is perceived by others.

Criteria	*Met*	*Not met at this time*
a. Participation in discussion reveals an understanding of congruency or discrepancies between questionnaires.	_____	_____
b. Analysis and evaluation comments demonstrate awareness of appropriate measures for dealing with perceived discrepancies or disclosed concerns.	_____	_____

Comments:

No Concerns _____   **Concerns** _____

Check **Concerns** if there are concerns related to student's self-perception **and/or** are expressed by the educational community.

Leon is a thirty-five year old male who has decided on a second career as an educator. He is extremely bright, articulate, and aggressively demanding. As a student in the classroom, he is a high achiever, outspoken, and often dominating. Although his written work is beautifully done, his fellow classmates are annoyed when working with him in cooperative groups. It is in this setting that his negative attitude and dispositions are most evident. It is Leon's way or no way. At least once a week, Leon makes an appointment with department personnel to complain or voice his opinion about other faculty, teachers in the field, his classmates, . . .

On paper, Leon is the ideal teacher candidate. In person, his attitude and his disposition paint an entirely different picture. Where and how can we weave our concerns about a student's attitude and dispositions into our assessment process?

Disposition and Attitude Questionnaires

Dispositions are trends in behavior that either foster or obstruct effective teaching. Previous assessments did not address the desire, commitment, or positive dispositions of the teacher candidate as necessary qualities for developing rational and caring teachers. Disposition questionnaires allow teacher candidates to reflect on their own attitudes and to see how they are perceived by faculty. This ultimately helps them understand not only the science of teaching, but also the art of teaching.

Teacher candidates are given four questionnaires during the orientation session. One questionnaire is for the teacher candidate and is written in first-person form. It is submitted with the application for Portfolio Presentation I. The candidate also must ask three faculty members in the college community to complete and return the questionnaires to the Education Department. Because students tend to choose faculty members with whom they have had positive experiences, the instructor of the prerequisite general methods course is required to submit a questionnaire on each and every student in the program. This process adds integrity to the attitude and disposition component.

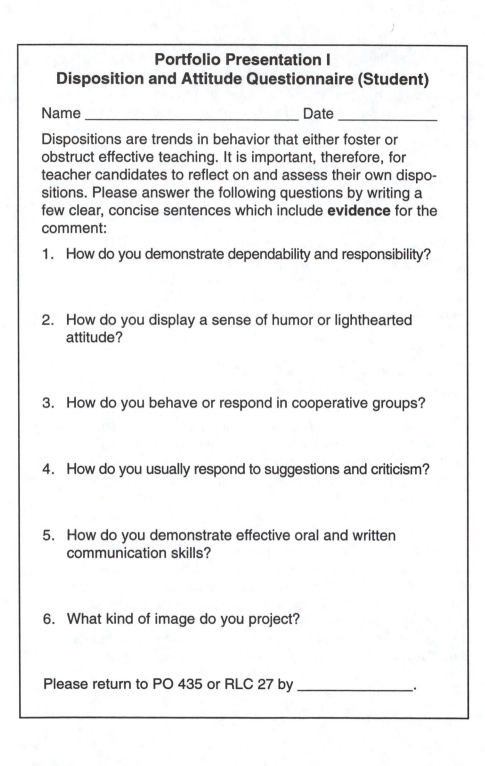

Portfolio Presentation I
Disposition and Attitude Questionnaire (Student)

Name _____ Date _____

Dispositions are trends in behavior that either foster or obstruct effective teaching. It is important, therefore, for teacher candidates to reflect on and assess their own dispositions. Please answer the following questions by writing a few clear, concise sentences which include **evidence** for the comment:

1. How do you demonstrate dependability and responsibility?

2. How do you display a sense of humor or lighthearted attitude?

3. How do you behave or respond in cooperative groups?

4. How do you usually respond to suggestions and criticism?

5. How do you demonstrate effective oral and written communication skills?

6. What kind of image do you project?

Please return to PO 435 or RLC 27 by _____.

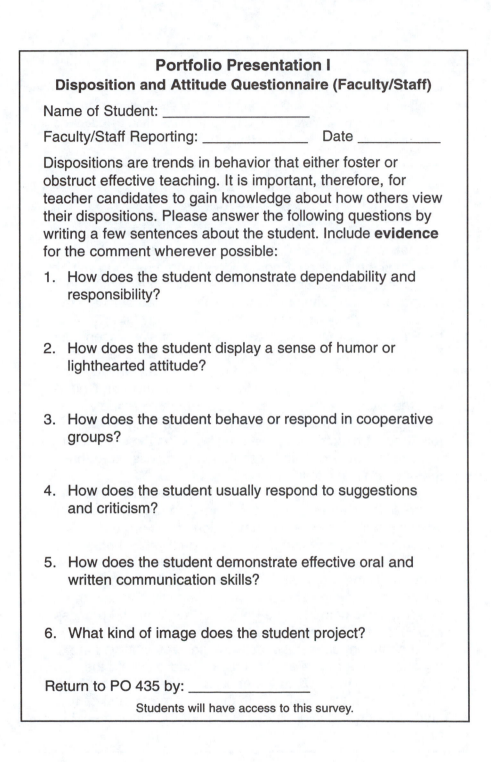

Portfolio Presentation I
Disposition and Attitude Questionnaire (Faculty/Staff)

Name of Student: _____

Faculty/Staff Reporting: _____   Date _____

Dispositions are trends in behavior that either foster or obstruct effective teaching. It is important, therefore, for teacher candidates to gain knowledge about how others view their dispositions. Please answer the following questions by writing a few sentences about the student. Include **evidence** for the comment wherever possible:

1. How does the student demonstrate dependability and responsibility?

2. How does the student display a sense of humor or lighthearted attitude?

3. How does the student behave or respond in cooperative groups?

4. How does the student usually respond to suggestions and criticism?

5. How does the student demonstrate effective oral and written communication skills?

6. What kind of image does the student project?

Return to PO 435 by: _____

Students will have access to this survey.

Appeal Process

For legal purposes, the Portfolio Presentation I Appeal Process is distributed and explained to all applicants during the orientation. Orientation leaders explain the proper procedure to follow in the event that a student does not meet the designated criteria to pass Portfolio Presentation I.

Portfolio Presentation I
Appeal Process

A student denied admittance to the Division of Teacher Education's Advanced Professional Sequence has the right to appeal the decision. Prior to scheduling a meeting with the Director of Teacher Education, the student must write a letter of appeal to the Teacher Education Committee outlining the rationale for reconsideration. The student may be invited by the Director of Teacher Education to personally present his/her case to the Teacher Education Committee. The decision of the committee will be given to the student in writing.

If the appeal is denied by the Teacher Education Committee, the student will be given an opportunity to reapply and complete the Portfolio Presentation I process again the following semester. No student will be given the opportunity to complete the Portfolio Presentation I process more than the one additional time.

A student who receives a 'pass with concerns' is required to meet with the designated facilitator and remove the stipulations within two weeks. If these stipulations are not satisfactorily removed by that date, the student will not pass Portfolio Presentation I. The student would be given the opportunity to reapply and complete Portfolio Presentation I again the following semester. No student will be given the opportunity to complete the Portfolio Presentation I process more than the one additional time.

If a student does not pass Portfolio Presentation I the second time, a further appeal may be addressed to the Associate Dean to whom the department reports. The Associate Dean, in consultation with the department, makes the final decision and informs the student of the outcome of his or her appeal.

Agenda

Two weekday evenings are set aside for portfolio presentations. All student applicants and faculty facilitators attend one of the two sessions. In order for the students to prepare for the evening's activities, a detailed agenda is given as part of the orientation. The agenda has the potential to raise or lower the teacher candidates' anxiety level. A sample agenda is shown below.

Portfolio Presentation I Agenda

Thursday Evening and Friday Evening 5:00–9:00 p.m.

Welcome

Introduction to Portfolio Presentation
> Purpose
> Overview of Session
> Announcement of Next Steps

Review criteria for current event
Students write on current issue while facilitators review students' office portfolios and disposition questionnaires.

Break

Present the Portfolios
Small group introductions from biographies with each student evaluating and then presenting his/her portfolio to the group. (Order of presentations determined by random drawing. Each presentation has a 15-minute maximum.)
> Student identifies strengths as seen in portfolio
> Student identifies areas of need as seen in portfolio
> Student identifies how faculty feedback has been used
> Student identifies goals for Advanced Professional Sequence
>   based upon evaluation of portfolio

Break

Review the Disposition Questionnaires
Students compare personal disposition questionnaires to those completed by faculty members, take notes, and prepare for interview.

Students individually interviewed
Identify similarities and differences between personal surveys and faculty surveys.

Large group discussion
Discuss the role of dispositions in effective teaching

Formal evaluation of Portfolio Presentation I

FACULTY FACILITATOR ORIENTATION SESSION

The facilitators are selected from among the full- and part-time faculty within the Teacher Education Division. Each semester approximately fifty students apply to participate in Portfolio Presentation I. This translates into twenty-five students for each of the two evening sessions. These twenty-five students are placed into five cohort groups of five students each with two facilitators assigned to each group. Facilitators are rotated each semester, and all faculty members are expected to participate at some time during the school year.

Orientations for faculty facilitators are conducted an hour before the evening sessions for Portfolio Presentation I. New or less experienced faculty facilitators are paired with seasoned facilitators who explain the evening's agenda and review rubrics for each of the four components to be evaluated. The teams of facilitators examine the office portfolios for students in their groups. This information is used to establish an academic profile which can be parlayed into discussion and interview questions. The orientation session ends with the facilitators being introduced to the large group of portfolio candidates.

THE PORTFOLIO PRESENTATION I SESSION

The four-hour evening session begins with a brief welcome by the Chair of Initial Certification. The purpose for the Portfolio Presentation and an overview of the four required components in the evening's session precedes students being assigned to their cohort groups.

Current Issue

The students are asked to write on their chosen issues to provide a writing sample and an update of the tracked subject. While the students are writing, the facilitators familiarize themselves with faculty and students' disposition questionnaires for each candidate assigned to their group.

Presentation of the Portfolio

Students are dispersed to one of five areas set aside for the cohort groups. To reduce what is by now a high level of anxiety and to establish a more relaxed environment, students are asked to introduce themselves using a portion of their personal narrative. The order of presentations is determined by a random drawing, and students are reminded that each presentation has a fifteen-minute maximum. The four features that need to be addressed by each student in their allotted time are:

- identified areas of strength as exhibited in the portfolio,
- identified areas of need,
- utilization of faculty feedback, and
- identified goals for advanced coursework.

This brief presentation is not simply a "show-and-tell" opportunity; it is designed to have the student reflect on the artifacts selected and to determine how those artifacts address their developing competencies as teachers.

A well-deserved break, complete with a light meal, follows this portion of the evening. While students relax, facilitators review the writing samples from the current issues. Criteria used to evaluate the work are:

- issue is clearly defined,
- impact of the issue on field of education and individual student is clearly stated, and
- writing is well-organized and has minimal usage errors.

Disposition and Attitude Questionnaires

As the students reconvene after the break, each person is given the attitude and disposition questionnaires that were completed by the faculty along with his or her own questionnaire previously submitted with the application. The students are given time to reflect and compare the proximity of the match between their perceptions of themselves and the way they are perceived by faculty. In a one-on-one interview, the teacher candidate reveals an understanding of the congruency or discrepancy between questionnaires. The candidate's analysis and evaluation comments must demonstrate an awareness of appropriate measures for dealing with perceived discrepancies or disclosed concerns.

As a closing activity, the facilitators of each small group conduct a brief discussion on how attitudes and personal dispositions either facilitate or inhibit one's ability to become an effective teacher and reflective decision maker. It is our intent to impress the students with the critical impact that attitudes and dispositions have upon the teaching profession.

Student Evaluation of Portfolio Presentation I

Before the candidates are dismissed, they are asked to complete an anonymous formal evaluation of the Portfolio Presentation I process. An example of a completed evaluation follows:

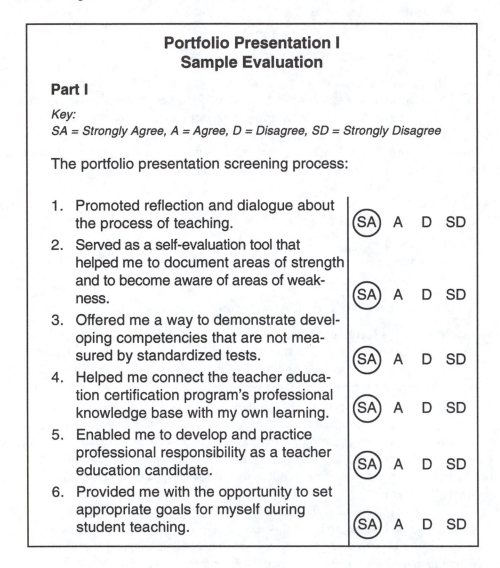

**Portfolio Presentation I
Sample Evaluation**

Part I

Key:
SA = Strongly Agree, A = Agree, D = Disagree, SD = Strongly Disagree

The portfolio presentation screening process:

1. Promoted reflection and dialogue about the process of teaching.   (SA) A   D SD

2. Served as a self-evaluation tool that helped me to document areas of strength and to become aware of areas of weakness.   (SA) A   D SD

3. Offered me a way to demonstrate developing competencies that are not measured by standardized tests.   (SA) A   D SD

4. Helped me connect the teacher education certification program's professional knowledge base with my own learning.   (SA) A   D SD

5. Enabled me to develop and practice professional responsibility as a teacher education candidate.   (SA) A   D SD

6. Provided me with the opportunity to set appropriate goals for myself during student teaching.   (SA) A   D SD

Part II

Which of these activities were personally beneficial and why?

1. Current Issue
   (Very Beneficial)   Beneficial   Less Beneficial

Why?
I enjoyed being able to write about my current issue, but I would have liked to have been able to bring in a topical paper. I would have been able to express my thoughts more fully.

2. Constructing the portfolio
   (Very Beneficial)   Beneficial   Less Beneficial

Why?
It helped me to think about the process of organization for my portfolio.

3. Presenting the portfolio
   (Very Beneficial)   Beneficial   Less Beneficial

Why?
I am a very verbal individual and it was fun to talk with my peers and hear what they learned about themselves and the profession.

4. Completing the personal disposition survey
   (Very Beneficial)   Beneficial   Less Beneficial

Why?
It made me really explore who I am as an individual and how I will relate to students in my classroom.

5. Comparing faculty input to personal disposition
   (Very Beneficial)   Beneficial   Less Beneficial

Why?
It was an extra boost for me to confirm my belief that I am right in my choice of becoming an elementary teacher.

General comments about Portfolio Presentation I
I really enjoyed putting the portfolio together even though it was quite challenging. I learned a lot about myself and my abilities.

ASSESSMENT BY THE FACILITATORS

After the student presentation portion of the evening is over, the facilitators spend time critically examining each candidate's portfolio. The student's developing competencies are ascertained by the following criteria:

- the portfolio meets or exceeds guidelines for appropriate artifacts in designated categories,
- each artifact in the portfolio has an accompanying explanation for its inclusion,
- a multicultural/diverse learner perspective is evident,
- contents display quality, and
- written contents display correct mechanical usage.

Throughout the portfolio presentation, facilitators have made notations on their worksheet rubrics for each of the four evaluated components. This information is utilized to complete the final report and recommendation to the Teacher Education Committee. This college-wide committee is the decision-making body that must approve each student's admittance to the advanced professional course work and student teaching.

Portfolio Presentation I
Outcomes/Assessment/Criteria

Student Name _____ Date _____

Facilitator Worksheet

1. The student will be able to demonstrate in writing his/her understanding of a pre-chosen educational issue.

Criteria	Met	Not met at this time
a. Issue has been clearly defined.	____	____
b. Impact of issue on the field of education and on the individual educator has been clearly stated.	____	____
c. Writing is well-organized and clear and has minimal usage errors.	____	____

Comments:

Pass ____   **Low Pass** ____   **No Pass** ____
All met: Pass   Mixture: Low Pass   No criteria met: No Pass

2. The student will be able to demonstrate to the educational community his/her developing competency through the compilation of a professional portfolio.

Criteria	Met	Not met at this time
a. Portfolio meets or exceeds written student guidelines for appropriate artifacts in designated categories.	_____	_____
b. Each artifact has accompanying explanation for its inclusion.	_____	_____
c. A multicultural/diverse learner perspective is evident.	_____	_____
d. Portfolio contents display quality and demonstrate developing competencies.	_____	_____
e. Portfolio contents display correct grammar, spelling, and punctuation.	_____	_____

Comments:

Pass _____   **Low Pass** _____   **No Pass** _____

All met: Pass   Mixture: Low Pass   No criteria met: No Pass

3. The student will be able to review the contents of his/her portfolio, express his/her analysis of the work, and set appropriate goals for his/her advanced professional sequence. (Presentation limited to 15 minutes.)

Criteria	*Met*	*Not met at this time*
a. Student identifies strengths of portfolio contents as they relate to becoming an effective teacher and reflective decision maker.	_____	_____
b. Student identifies areas of the portfolio contents where support and time are needed.	_____	_____
c. Student identifies how he/she has followed through on faculty feedback to date.	_____	_____
d. Student identifies goals to pursue during course work in the advanced professional sequence.	_____	_____

Comments:

Pass _____   **Low Pass** _____   **No Pass** _____

All met: Pass   Mixture: Low Pass   No criteria met: No Pass

4. The student will be able to provide the educational community with information regarding the proximity of the match between the student's perception of his/her personal dispositions and the way the student is perceived by others.

Criteria	*Met*	*Not met at this time*
a. Participation in discussion reveals an understanding of congruency or discrepancies between questionnaires.	_____	_____
b. Analysis and evaluation comments demonstrate awareness of appropriate measures for dealing with perceived discrepancies or disclosed concerns.	_____	_____

Concerns:

No Concerns _____   Concerns _____

Discussion Question

How do your attitudes and personal dispositions either facilitate or inhibit your ability to become an effective teacher and reflective decision maker?

Facilitator's signature _____

FINAL REPORT AND RECOMMENDATION

Each of the four components are evaluated on a "pass," "low pass," or "no pass" format based on the rubrics. Because students have access to the Final Report form, facilitators provide comments as feedback.

Portfolio Presentation I
Final Report for _____
(Student Name)

1. Educational Issue
   Pass _____   Low Pass _____   No Pass _____
   Comments:

2. Compilation of Portfolio
   Pass _____   Low Pass _____   No Pass _____
   Comments:

3. Presentation of Portfolio
   Pass _____   Low Pass _____   No Pass _____
   Comments:

4. Disposition Questionnaire
   No Concerns _____   Concerns _____
   Comments:

Recommendation to Teacher Education Committee

Pass _____   Low Pass _____   No Pass _____
(All pass, no concerns) (Any combination with   (No Pass in # 2
                         stipulations)   &/or #3)

Comments:

Stipulations

If low pass in: 1. Rewrite   If no pass in: 1. Conference and rewrite
                2. Redo   2. Next semester with new
                                                   portfolio
                3. Re-present   3. Next semester with new
                                                   presentation
                4. Conference   4. Conference and contract

Signatures: _____   Date: _____
            _____   Date: _____

Students will have access to this form.

The facilitator's recommendation to the Teacher Education Committee is based on evaluation of the four components of the three possible recommendations—pass, low pass, no pass—if the recommendation is:

- Pass, the committee approves the student's admission to the advanced professional sequence, which allows the student to take upper-level course work.

- Low pass, the student is given stipulations to fulfill within a specified time. The stipulations must be validated by the facilitator in order to pass at a later date. If the student received a low pass in the area of the disposition questionnaire, they must confer with the department chair regarding inconsistencies. The conference results in a written plan that documents how the student will resolve this problem.

- No pass, the student must reapply and participate in the presentation process the following semester.

The teacher candidates receive written notification from the Director of Teacher Education as to the decision of the committee. Copies of the decision and Portfolio Presentation I paperwork are placed in the student's office portfolio.

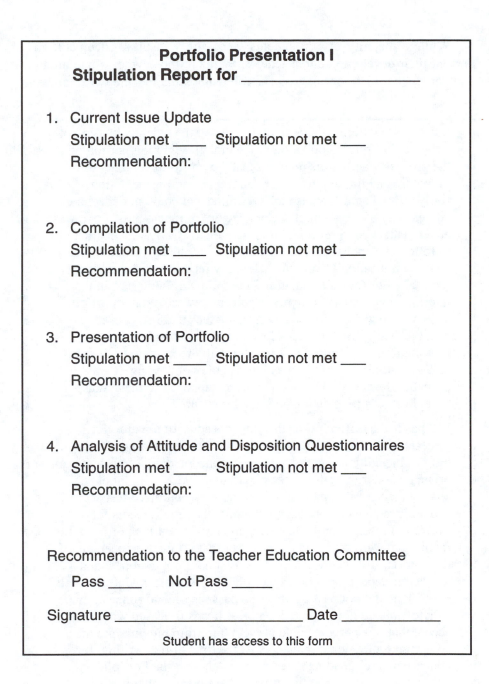

Portfolio Presentation I
Stipulation Report for _____

1. Current Issue Update
   Stipulation met _____ Stipulation not met ___
   Recommendation:

2. Compilation of Portfolio
   Stipulation met _____ Stipulation not met ___
   Recommendation:

3. Presentation of Portfolio
   Stipulation met _____ Stipulation not met ___
   Recommendation:

4. Analysis of Attitude and Disposition Questionnaires
   Stipulation met _____ Stipulation not met ___
   Recommendation:

Recommendation to the Teacher Education Committee
   Pass _____   Not Pass _____

Signature _____ Date _____

Student has access to this form

While a majority of our students successfully display, document, and present their developing competencies, there are those who in one area or another receive a low or no pass. The following scenarios are two examples of the latter.

Carly is a traditional undergraduate education student who did not pass the portfolio compilation or the oral presentation portion of the process. Facilitators reported that the portfolio contents were immature and limited in variety. During her oral presentation, Carly fixated on a "woe is me" syndrome and could not adequately address any of her strengths. Upon receipt of the no pass, there was anger, tearful conferences, and upset parents. Carly was instructed to follow the appeal process, which was eventually denied by the Teacher Education Committee. Her only recourse at that time was to re-take Portfolio Presentation I the following semester. In the intermittent months, Carly revamped and revitalized her portfolio and came to grips with some personal issues that had caused her some difficulty. She was able to successfully complete Portfolio Presentation I the following semester with this comment: "I can honestly admit that as upset as I was about not passing, it was probably the best thing that could have happened to me at that time. I faced some tough issues and I grew up."

Bill has had a difficult time deciding his education major. Each semester during advising, he has chosen a different area of concentration. In addition, faculty have been concerned about his inappropriate behavior in both college classrooms and K–12 school environments. Bill's grade point average, standardized test scores, and college course work adequately met the requirements for Portfolio Presentation I. However, upon review of his portfolio, the facilitators were astounded to discover that it failed to meet any of the criteria. Bill received a no pass. He chose not to appeal and decided to repeat the process the following semester. Unfortunately for Bill, he did not pass again. A no pass the second time automatically dismissed him from the major. Bill was livid and would not accept that this process could prevent him from moving into the advanced professional sequence. At the time of this writing, further appeals are still pending. We are confident that the Portfolio Process will stand up to litigation and are pleased that it has accomplished what it was meant to do.

PORTFOLIO PRESENTATION II

After successfully implementing Portfolio Presentation I for two semesters, we were excited to begin piloting the second phase of the process, Portfolio Presentation II. There were several questions and comments brought forward by students at that point in time.

"I didn't do Portfolio I because I went through Decision Making Seminar. Why do I have to do Portfolio II?"

"If I don't pass, will this really keep me from student teaching?"

"How is this different from Portfolio Presentation I?"

"Will principals and cooperating teachers want to see my portfolio?"

"Why do I have to do an interview? I did one with career services."

"I learned so much from doing Portfolio Presentation I. I'm excited to participate in this process."

"Can't I just turn in the same portfolio that I did for Portfolio Presentation I?"

"I'm excited about a faculty member spending quality time with me to make suggestions about my portfolio."

GRAPHIC ORGANIZER FOR PORTFOLIO PRESENTATION II

Rationale
Methodology
Student Orientation Sessions
    Requirements
    Application Forms
    Calendar
    Office Portfolio
    Portfolio Organization Guidelines

Outcomes/Assessment/Criteria
Appeal Process
Interviewer Orientation Sessions
Portfolio Presentation II Session
Week One: Portfolios Due
Week Two: Interviews
Week Three: Conferences with Review Board Members
Review Board Caucus

RATIONALE

The semester prior to student teaching, the teacher candidates must participate in, and successfully pass, a second screening process known as Portfolio Presentation II. This makes them eligible to student teach. Formerly, the application for student teaching was simply a paper screening with three letters of recommendation from college faculty. The old process was neither real-world based nor helpful to the teacher candidates or faculty. As with Portfolio Presentation I, a few students were able to qualify despite concerns from faculty and/or field experience evaluations.

METHODOLOGY

Portfolio Presentation II was designed with three major objectives in mind:

- To review and culminate preparatory course work and experiences,
- To provide evidence of competency for student teaching, and
- To tie the portfolio criteria to real-world expectations.

In order to accomplish the first and second objectives, the teacher candidates need to update, refine, and polish their portfolios. They also are required to write a thorough analysis of their portfolio to demonstrate their ability as a reflective decision maker. The third objective is accomplished by having each student participate in a mock job interview with a faculty member. The final step in this process is a one-on-one critique and oral defense of the portfolio.

STUDENT ORIENTATION SESSIONS

Once the dates for the Portfolio Presentation II Orientation Sessions have been established, they are listed in the education calendar and posted for student notification. Students must attend one of several sessions, each lasting approximately an hour. Orientations are generally held within the first few weeks of the semester, with interviews and portfolio defenses scheduled within the month. Teacher candidates receive application materials and guidelines at the orientation meeting. The remainder of this section will briefly describe each of these.

Requirements

The Director of Student Teaching conducts the orientation sessions, which present an overview of the process and a reminder of the prerequisites for the application to student teaching. Any candidates who have not completed the prerequisites or have not met all requirements may not apply for Portfolio Presentation II, which is admission to student teaching.

Portfolio Presentation II
Requirements

Applicants must:

1. Pass Portfolio Presentation I
2. Pass all sections of PPST/ Praxis I
3. Earn an overall and education GPA of at least 3.0
4. Earn a content GPA of at least 3.0
5. Receive a minimum grade of B- in English 101, English 102 and Communication Arts 101
6. Complete all courses listed as Major Professional Requirements with a grade of C or better (effective fall 1996)
7. Complete or be enrolled in Ed/SEd 300: Clinical Placement
8. Complete at least 15 credits (PBC) or 21 credits (transfers). Transcripts for all courses completed off-campus must be submitted
9. Complete and register all Credit for Prior Learning credits
10. Prepare portfolio for submission

Application Forms

The application form is completed by the teacher candidate and is used to verify the student's candidacy. The form also allows the student to list various suggestions for student teaching placements, although candidates are not guaranteed a placement at these suggested schools. Completing the application process does not guarantee that a candidate will be allowed to student teach; interviews and defenses must be passed before placements are processed. In addition to the application form, other paperwork must be submitted that is critical in preparation for student teaching, but not part of the portfolio process.

Portfolio Presentation II
Application

Name _____ Student ID Number _____

Address _____

Phone Number _____

Certification Area: Major _____ Certifiable Minor _____
                                                                (if applicable)

Status: Traditional _____   PBC ____

Clinical Status:
    I have completed Ed/SEd 300 ____
    I am presently enrolled in Ed/SEd 300 ____

I have successfully completed the Pre-Professional Skills Test/ Praxis I:

Reading: Score ____ Mathematics: Score ____ Writing: Score ____
Date _____   Date _____   Date _____

Student teaching placements: I will require ___ placements
                                                              number

Suggested Placements

Placement 1:   School _____
                Teacher _____ Gr/Subject _____
Placement 2:   School _____
                Teacher _____ Gr/Subject _____
Placement 3:   School _____
                Teacher _____ Gr/Subject _____

List of interviewers will be posted on the information board across from RLC 27. Find your designated interviewer and contact him/her to arrange an interview date. This is your responsibility. You must complete the arrangement and the interview before _____ or this application will be null and void.

Calendar

Students are presented with a calendar outlining the procedures for application, interview, and defense. The timeline is a reminder to the candidates of the critical due dates in the Portfolio Presentation II process.

Portfolio Presentation II
Sample Calendar

February 7	Application materials due in RLC 27.
Week of February 10	Interviewers' and reviewers' names and sign-up sheets will be posted. Sign up for an appointment with each.
Week of February 17	Conference with your interviewer on the designated date at the designated time.
February 21	Portfolios due to your reviewer.
Week of March 3	Conference with your reviewer regarding your portfolio on the designated date at the designated time.
March 14	Review Board Members' recommendations presented to the Teacher Education Committee.

Placement process will begin after approval has been given by the Teacher Education Committee.

Office Portfolio

The student's office portfolio is updated to include additional clinical evaluations and test scores, current grade point average, and pertinent course work. The office portfolio is used to ensure that students have met all requirements.

Portfolio Presentation II
Office Portfolio

Name _____   Undergraduate _____
                                PBC _____
Date of Portfolio Presentation I: _____

PPST/Praxis I   Writing   Reading   Mathematics
    Score   _____   _____   _____
    Date Passed _____   _____   _____

    GPA   Overall _____   Education _____

Transcript for Portfolio Presentation II _____

Clinical Evaluations for Ed/SEd 300
    No Concerns _____   Concerns _____

Undergraduates only:

Required grades approved for Portfolio Presentation I _____

or

Grades for: En 101 _____   En 102 _____   CA 101 _____

Port II Facilitators' Recommendation:
Pass _____ Pass with Concerns _____ Deny _____

Port II TEC's Recommendation:
Pass _____ Pass with Concerns _____ Deny _____

Date _____

Portfolio Organization Guidelines

The guidelines remain consistent with Portfolio Presentation I: Students organize their portfolio contents according to the seven categories of the knowledge base. The diversity/multicultural component remains an important focus that must be evident throughout the artifacts.

Outcomes/Assessment/Criteria

There are three components to Portfolio Presentation II. Students will be assessed according to specific criteria for each of these three areas:

1. Portfolio contents. Portfolios are evaluated according to appropriateness of artifacts and rationale for inclusion. A professional and market-ready appearance is essential.

2. Analysis of portfolio. A polished, professionally written reflection that includes information on student's strengths, faculty feedback, and identified goals for student teaching is required.

3. Interview. Students participate in a one-on-one interview and respond to student teaching case scenarios with appropriate and positive solutions.

Portfolio Presentation II
Outcomes/Assessment/Criteria
Student Orientation

1. The student will demonstrate to the educational community his/her competency through the compilation of a portfolio.

Criteria	*Met*	*Not met at this time*
a. Portfolio meets or exceeds written student guidelines for appropriate artifacts in designated categories.	_____	_____
b. Each artifact has accompanying explanation for its inclusion.	_____	_____
c. A multicultural/diverse learner perspective is evident.	_____	_____
d. Portfolio contents display quality and demonstrate developing competencies.	_____	_____
e. Appearance of portfolio is professional and market-ready for intended certification.	_____	_____

Comments:

Pass _____   **Low Pass** _____   **No Pass** _____
All met: Pass   One or two criteria   Three or more criteria
                     not met: Low Pass   not met: No Pass

2. The student will submit a typed analysis of his/her portfolio and appropriate goals for student teaching.

	Criteria	*Met*	*Not met at this time*
a.	Student identifies strengths of portfolio contents as they relate to becoming an effective student teacher and reflective decision maker.	_____	_____
b.	Student identifies how faculty feedback has been utilized during the advanced professional course work.	_____	_____
c.	Student identifies goals to pursue during student teaching.	_____	_____
d.	Student's work demonstrates a professional appearance.	_____	_____

Comments:

Pass _____   **Low Pass** _____   **No Pass** _____

All met: Pass   One or two criteria not met: Low Pass   Three or more criteria not met: No Pass

3. The student will demonstrate developing professionalism by participating in a one-on-one interview.

Criteria	*Met*	*Not met at this time*
a. Student responds to student teaching case scenarios with appropriate and positive solutions.	_____	_____
b. Student clearly and effectively articulates responses to student teaching case scenarios.	_____	_____
c. Student presents himself/ herself in a poised, professional manner.	_____	_____
d. Student initiated and facilitated interview process in a timely and responsible manner.	_____	_____

Comments:

Pass _____   **Low Pass** _____   **No Pass** _____

All met: Pass   One or two criteria not met: Low Pass   Three or more criteria not met: No Pass

Appeal Process

During the orientation, the Portfolio Presentation II Appeal Process is distributed and explained to all applicants. The process is the same in Portfolio Presentation I and II. Not passing Portfolio Presentation II means that a student would not be able to register for the following semester because the only remaining certification requirement is student teaching.

Portfolio Presentation II
Appeal Process

A student denied admittance to Student Teaching has the right to appeal the decision. Prior to scheduling a meeting with the Director of Teacher Education, the student must submit an appeal letter to the Teacher Education Committee outlining the rationale for reconsideration.

A student may be given an opportunity to reapply and complete the Portfolio Presentation II process again the following semester. No student will be given the opportunity to complete the Portfolio Presentation II process more than one additional time.

A further appeal must be addressed to the Associate Dean to whom the department reports. The Associate Dean, in consultation with the department, makes the final decision and informs the student of the outcome of his/her appeal.

INTERVIEWER ORIENTATION SESSIONS

A four-member review board has responsibility for facilitating Portfolio Presentation II. In addition to conducting the orientation session for students, each reviewer provides individual training for the faculty interviewers. Sessions are scheduled during which the reviewer and the interviewer discuss paperwork and procedures to be followed during the one-on-one interview sessions. College faculty who will be conducting the one-on-one interviews are given the interview format specifying the questions to be asked. Each candidate is asked the same set of opening questions for consistency and equity.

Along with the questions, a menu of twenty student teaching scenarios is offered to the interviewer from which the interviewer will choose three to pose to the candidate for response. Some scenarios are more specific to particular certification levels; the menu provides latitude for choices appropriate to the candidate. Where consistency and equity are important for one portion of the interview, the necessity to determine how well the candidates are able to think on their feet is another critical attribute in this, as in any, authentic interview. The fact that each interviewer has a wide selection of scenarios from which to choose, limits the possibility of students receiving advanced information which would allow them to prepare a response. All of the scenarios have been drawn from authentic student teaching placements. The following are examples of two scenarios that could be used in the interview.

You have a very good friend coming into town who you have not seen in a long time. You have decided to call in sick to your student teaching placement so you can spend the day with your friend. While having lunch in a restaurant, you are greeted by your college supervisor's secretary. What would you do next?

As a student teacher you have been placed in a very difficult situation. Your cooperating teacher, in your presence, has physically and verbally mistreated a student. The next day, the school principal comes to talk with the cooperating teacher in response to a parental phone call regarding this situation. Again, in your presence, the cooperating teacher totally denies that the situation ever occurred. What do you do now?

Portfolio Presentation II
Interview Format

Interviewer: _____ Date _____

Student: _____

Please ask the student each of the following questions. Briefly record the student's response and any comments you may have regarding the response.

1. Briefly share what you would like me to know about you.

2. *If not previously answered . . .*
    a. What is your certification area?

    b. How have your experiences with children or young adults prepared you for student teaching?

3. What are your short-term and long-term goals?

4. Briefly share your philosophy of education.

5. Share what you feel your strengths and weaknesses are related to becoming a teacher.

After you give the student the three scenario questions, please ask this final question and record the student's response.

6. Is there anything you'd like to share or ask that has not yet been discussed?

To reinforce the interviewer's decision, particularly when a teacher candidate does not perform well, the session is recorded. All students are informed during the orientation session that the interviews are recorded. Tape recorders and tapes are provided. Interviewer comments regarding the teacher candidate's reaction to the scenarios and the rubric remarks for the total interview session are recorded on the Interviewer's Response Form. Interviewers are instructed to return all materials to the review board members upon completion of the interviews.

Portfolio Presentation II
Interviewer Response Form

Interviewer _____

Student _____

Please use this form to record scenario responses and comments.

Scenario # ____:

Scenario # ____:

Scenario # ____:

Interviewer's overall comments and recommendations:

Pass _____   Low Pass _____   No Pass _____

Interviewer's signature _____ Date _____

Information from this form may be shared with the student.

PORTFOLIO PRESENTATION II SESSION

Portfolio Presentation II is a three-week process. The week following the Portfolio Presentation Student Orientation, application materials are due in the office of the Director of Student Teaching. The Director assumes the responsibility for coordinating all aspects of Portfolio Presentation II, which include random assignments of teacher candidates to both a reviewer and an interviewer. Reviewers, members of the four-person Review Board, include the Chair of Initial Certification, the Director of Student Teaching, and two initial certification faculty. The responsibility of each reviewer is to oversee a number of applicants and to facilitate the process for each one. The interviewers are selected from Division of Teacher Education faculty at large; several interviewers work with each reviewer.

Week One: Portfolios Due

Candidates must submit their professional, market-ready portfolios to their assigned reviewers. The timeframe allows the reviewer two weeks to read and react to each portfolio. Although students do not make an oral portfolio presentation, they are required to submit an analysis with the portfolio. This provides the reviewers with the opportunity to assess writing skills and student understanding and internalization of the knowledge base. The rubrics designated on the Reviewer Worksheet are utilized in this assessment process.

Week Two: Interviews

Interviewers have posted available appointment times for the interview week. Candidates choose an available time slot and assume the responsibility of verifying the appointment with the interviewer. Teacher candidates are expected to arrive promptly and dress professionally for their interviews. Following the interview, faculty return completed rubrics, tapes, and recorders to their reviewer. Although review board members have the responsibility for processing the results of Portfolio Presentation II with each candidate, teacher education faculty conduct the actual interviews. Faculty have shared comments with us concerning their involvement in this process:

> "As an instructor who normally works with graduate students, it was delightful to meet some initial certification candidates and hear what they believe about teaching."
>
> "Make sure you keep me on the list for next semester. I enjoyed this."
>
> "The students' appearance and deportment were most impressive."
>
> "The interview process operates very smoothly."

Week Three: Conferences With Review Board Members

The purpose of this conference is to convey the interviewer's and reviewer's reactions and comments to the teacher candidate. If concerns are expressed, the student is expected to professionally defend the point in question. This one-hour conference also provides detailed feedback to the student for refinement of the portfolio as a marketing tool. Components of the three-week portfolio session are reviewed, and a final, culminating report is written and shared with the candidate. At the end of the conference, the candidate is asked to complete and return an evaluation form for the Portfolio II process.

Portfolio Presentation II
Outcomes/Assessment/Criteria

Review Board Member Worksheet

1. The student will demonstrate to the educational community his/her competency through the compilation of a portfolio.

Criteria	*Met*	*Not met at this time*
a. Portfolio meets or exceeds written student guidelines for appropriate artifacts in designated categories.	_____	_____
b. Each artifact has accompanying explanation for its inclusion.	_____	_____
c. A multicultural/diverse learner perspective is evident.	_____	_____
d. Appearance of portfolio is professional and market-ready for intended certification.	_____	_____

Comments:

Pass _____   **Low Pass** _____   **No Pass** _____

All met: Pass   One or two criteria not met: Low Pass   Three or more criteria not met: No Pass

2. The student will submit a typed analysis of his/her portfolio and appropriate goals for student teaching.

Criteria	Met	Not met at this time
a. Student identifies strengths of portfolio contents as they relate to becoming an effective student teacher and reflective decision maker.	_____	_____
b. Student identifies how faculty feedback has been utilized during the advanced professional course work.	_____	_____
c. Student identifies goals to pursue during student teaching.	_____	_____
d. Student work demonstrates a professional appearance.	_____	_____

Comments:

Pass _____   **Low Pass** _____   **No Pass** _____
All met: Pass   One or two criteria   Three or more criteria
                  not met: Low Pass   not met: No Pass

3. The student will be able to demonstrate developing professionalism by participating in a one-on-one interview.

	Criteria	*Met*	*Not met at this time*
a.	Student responds to student teaching case scenarios with appropriate and positive solutions.	_____	_____
b.	Student clearly and effectively articulates those responses.	_____	_____
c.	Student presents himself/herself in a poised, professional manner.	_____	_____
d.	Student initiated and facilitated interview process in a timely and responsible manner.	_____	_____

Comments:

Pass _____   **Low Pass** _____   **No Pass** _____

| All met: Pass | One or two criteria not met: Low Pass | Three or more criteria not met: No Pass |

Portfolio Presentation II
Final Report for _____
(Student Name)

1. Compilation/contents of portfolio
   Pass _____   Low Pass _____   No Pass _____
   Comments:

2. Analysis of portfolio and setting of appropriate goals
   Pass _____   Low Pass _____   No Pass _____
   Comments:

3. Interview
   Pass _____   Low Pass _____   No Pass _____
   Comments:

Recommendation to Teacher Education Committee
All Pass _____   Low Pass _____   No Pass _____
                           1.   Low Pass   1.   No Pass
                           2/3. Low or No Pass   2/3. No Pass
Comments:

Stipulations

If Low Pass in: 1. Redo desig-   If No Pass in: 1. Redo Port II next
                   nated criteria   semester
                2. Rewrite   2. Rewrite and conference
                3. Get feedback   3. Committee review of
                   from interviewer   audiotape

Signatures: _____   Date: _____

Students will have access to this form.

Portfolio Presentation II
Stipulation Report for _____

1. Compilation/Contents of portfolio:
    Stipulation met _____ Stipulation not met _____
    Recommendation:

2. Analysis of portfolio and setting of appropriate goals:
    Stipulation met _____ Stipulation not met _____
    Recommendation:

3. Interview:
    Stipulation met _____ Stipulation not met _____
    Recommendation:

Recommendation to the Teacher Education Committee

    Pass _____   No Pass _____

Signature _____ Date _____

Student has access to this form.

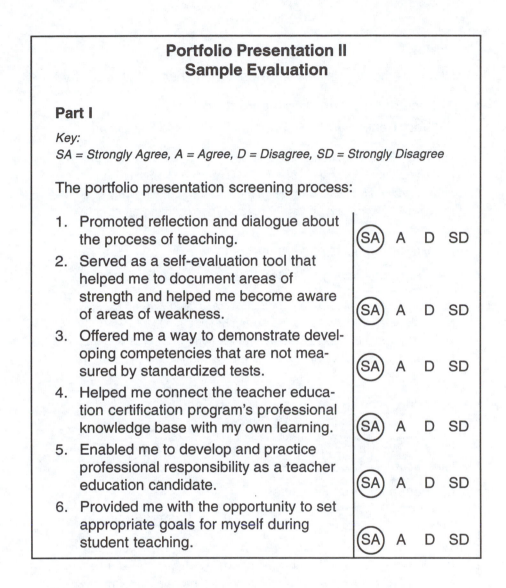

Portfolio Presentation II
Sample Evaluation

Part I

Key:
SA = Strongly Agree, A = Agree, D = Disagree, SD = Strongly Disagree

The portfolio presentation screening process:

1. Promoted reflection and dialogue about the process of teaching.   (SA) A   D   SD

2. Served as a self-evaluation tool that helped me to document areas of strength and helped me become aware of areas of weakness.   (SA) A   D   SD

3. Offered me a way to demonstrate developing competencies that are not measured by standardized tests.   (SA) A   D   SD

4. Helped me connect the teacher education certification program's professional knowledge base with my own learning.   (SA) A   D   SD

5. Enabled me to develop and practice professional responsibility as a teacher education candidate.   (SA) A   D   SD

6. Provided me with the opportunity to set appropriate goals for myself during student teaching.   (SA) A   D   SD

Part II

Which of these activities were personally beneficial and why?

1. Constructing/Compiling the Portfolio

   (Very Beneficial)   Beneficial   Less Beneficial

Why?   I have been compiling artifacts of my work for four years but there was no sense of order. Constructing the portfolio not only provided the necessary sequence, but also concretely showed me that I have gained the skills needed for becoming an effective teacher.

2. Writen Analysis of Portfolio

   (Very Beneficial)   Beneficial   Less Beneficial

Why?   Reflection is always beneficial, and this was no exception. Not only was I able to identify strengths, but also areas I would like to improve in the future. Also helpful was the writing of the goals. I have many goals, but this exercise forced me to identify and order those goals.

3. Interview with Teacher Education Faculty

   (Very Beneficial)   Beneficial   Less Beneficial

Why?   I was in the previous program before Portfolio I was implemented, so I was excused from this portion of Portfolio II.

4. Feedback from Reviewer

   (Very Beneficial)   Beneficial   Less Beneficial

Why?   When you work on something for a long time, you tend to lose your perspective. Feedback from the Reviewer offers a "fresh look" and also gave me a glimpse of what a prospective employer would see.

General comments about Portfolio Presentation II

Wonderful, great, helpful, insightful, beneficial!!!
Creating a portfolio is something I needed to do before I enter the job search market. I am thankful that the Education Department offered guidelines and assistance because I didn't have a clue on how to go about it.

Review Board Caucus

The four members of the review board meet to discuss the portfolios, stipulations, and recommendations made to the Teacher Education Committee. Once the recommendations have been voted on by the committee, the Director of Teacher Education writes the candidate regarding the decision. Copies of this decision and Portfolio Presentation II paperwork are added to the student's office portfolio.

The list of candidates admitted to student teaching is forwarded to the Director of Student Teaching, and the process for placing the candidates in the field can now begin. As our reputation for the portfolio process spreads, it becomes easier to procure student teaching and internship placements in area pre-K–12 schools. Many positive comments have come from principals and cooperative teachers regarding the portfolio process and the portfolios themselves.

> The principal of one of our frequently used student teaching sites has been most complimentary. He feels that the portfolios have helped polish the teacher candidates and has better prepared them for dialogue about educational practices. He makes a point of reviewing each student teacher's portfolio and talks with them about it. As a humorous aside, he told us he had requested a portfolio from a student teacher who attends another teacher preparation college in the area. The student responded, "A what?"

PORTFOLIO PRESENTATION III

One of our student teachers recounted the following story regarding Mary, her niece.

> Mary, a very competent teacher candidate from a nearby university, has had difficulty obtaining a teaching position. Due to her strong recommendations and academic file, she is frequently granted interviews but has been unable to secure a position. In a debriefing conference with a school principal where she was second choice, Mary was told the reason she was not selected. She and the other candidate were equally qualified across the board; the other candidate had a portfolio, Mary did not.

GRAPHIC ORGANIZER FOR PORTFOLIO PRESENTATION III

Rationale
Methodology
Student Orientation Session
Preparation for Portfolio Presentation III
Portfolio Presentation III Session

RATIONALE

Portfolio Presentation III is designated as admission to the teaching profession. It is a culminating experience designed to celebrate the completion of the candidates' program and provides a venue to display their portfolios to members of the educational community. Administrators from the many surrounding districts value the opportunity to meet the candidates, gather resumes, peruse portfolios, and talk informally with prospective hires.

METHODOLOGY

Teacher candidates are excused from their student teaching placements to attend a full-day Portfolio Presentation III session. Five major objectives are met during this time:

- to provide a forum for discussion related to student teaching experiences, hopes, fears, goals, dreams . . .

- to fulfill the Department of Public Instruction's requirement regarding the human relations component,

- to provide information and application for licensure and job search hints,

- to introduce Project First Year Initiative (Project FYI), a supportive mentoring network for beginning teachers, and

- to bridge the candidate's preservice training to the profession and provide exposure to hiring personnel in the K–12 community

STUDENT ORIENTATION SESSION

At the beginning of each semester, student teachers attend an orientation meeting. A memo and an agenda provide the teacher candidates with pertinent information regarding Portfolio Presentation III.

Portfolio Presentation III
Sample Memo

To: All Initial Certification Student Teachers
From: Initial Certification Faculty
Date: August 26, 1997
RE: Portfolio Presentation III

Portfolio Presentation III has been instituted to provide an informal opportunity for each of you to show off your portfolio and meet the hiring personnel from the greater Milwaukee area. It is a time to celebrate the completion of your program and the beginning of your career as a teacher. It is assumed that you have been continually upgrading and refining your portfolio since the last presentation. You should have many wonderful additions from your student teaching experiences to share with the K–12 community.

Portfolio Presentation III will be held on December 5, 1997; attendance is a mandatory prerequisite for certification. You will be excused from your second quarter student teaching placement for these activities. An agenda is enclosed for your reference.

Administrators from the surrounding communities will be present during the afternoon session held in the fieldhouse. You will be seated at tables according to your certification levels, and your portfolio will be available for perusal. Each of you should have with you several copies of your resume for distribution if requested. Please dress professionally as this may garner a possible interview at a later date.

Please note that all undergraduate certification candidates must be present at 9:30 a.m. to take the exit exam for accreditation. This is not a test for which you need to study; it is a test of general knowledge that is required by the North Central Accreditation Agency for all university graduates. You must be prompt!

Initial certification candidates who are not undergraduates (PBCs) will not need to take the exam, but must be present by 11:00 a.m. for the opening activities prior to a celebratory luncheon. During dessert and coffee, we will recognize our PBC students since they do not have a graduation ceremony.

Make certain that you put this date on your calendar NOW! We look forward to seeing all of you at this special function.

Portfolio Presentation III
Agenda

9:30 a.m.   Academic Profile (undergrads only)
                    Auditorium
11:00 a.m.   Opening Activity
                    Cardinal Lounge
11:30 a.m.   Celebration Luncheon
                    PBC Recognition
                    Serra Hall
12:15 p.m.   Information Sharing
                    Cardinal Lounge
                        Application for Certification
                        Job Search Hints
                        First Year Initiative
                        Alumni News
                        Cap and Gown Distribution
1:15 p.m.   Break
1:30 p.m.   Portfolio Presentation III
                    Fieldhouse
3:00 p.m.   Dismissal

PREPARATION FOR
PORTFOLIO PRESENTATION III

At mid-semester, a letter is sent to cooperating teachers requesting that they excuse the teacher candidates from regular classroom duties to allow them to attend Portfolio Presentation III. At the same time, an invitation is issued to a large number of area administrators asking them to participate in the day's activities.

Portfolio Presentation III
Sample Letter to Cooperating Teachers

Dear Cooperating Teacher,

On December 5, 1997, the faculty and initial certification candidates from the College of Education will hold its semi-annual Portfolio Presentation and Celebration. The presentation is designed to bridge the candidate's preservice training to the profession and to provide exposure to hiring personnel in the K–12 community. We are requesting that your student teacher be excused from his/her placement on this day as **attendance is a mandatory prerequisite for Wisconsin certification.** An agenda is enclosed for your information and interest.

If you have not seen your student teacher's portfolio to date, you may want to request an opportunity to review it. Your input would be most valuable to the student in preparation for this presentation.

Any comments or questions should be addressed to _____.

We appreciate your cooperation, and thank you for excusing your student teacher from his/her classroom responsibilities for that day.

Portfolio Presentation III
Sample Invitation

The faculty and graduates of the College of Education cordially request the honor of your presence at our first semiannual Portfolio Presentation and Celebration.

What: Our celebration provides you with an informal opportunity to meet our graduating teacher candidates and browse through their portfolios.

How: The prospective teachers will be seated according to certification areas; will have resumes available, and will answer any questions you may have.

Why: The presentation is designed to bridge the candidate's preservice training to the profession and provide exposure to hiring personnel in the K–12 community.

When: Friday, December 5

1:30–3:00 p.m.

Where: University Fieldhouse

Refreshments will be served

RSVP/questions to:

PORTFOLIO PRESENTATION III SESSION

Portfolio Presentation III begins with a collegial exchange where, for example, teacher candidates would share two accomplishments—one personal and one professional—from their student teaching experience. The comments generated range from serious reflection to humorous anecdotes. The discussion then evolves into a series of well-directed questions that pertain to human relation skills and how they are utilized with children and adults.

Next on the agenda is a celebration luncheon designed to honor all students completing graduation and/or certification requirements. An hour is set aside after lunch for disseminating logistical information. This generally includes licensure applications, job search hints, and alumni news.

A portion of this time is delegated to providing information about the college's First Year Initiative Project (Project FYI), a multifaceted support program for beginning teachers developed and implemented by two Initial Certification faculty. Various services provided by Project FYI include:

- a resource room housing units, learning centers, and instructional resources,
- grade-level cohort groups for first-, second-, and third-year teachers,
- a help-line for quick response to immediate concerns,
- classroom observations with feedback/support upon request,
- a newsletter, and
- regular socials/get-togethers.

In addition, the two college implementors are in direct contact with the administrators who have hired our graduates as first year teachers. Because of Project FYI, these first year teachers have often been referred to as "teachers with a warranty." Postcards with the title "Yippee! I'm employed!" are distributed to the students with instructions to return them to us as soon as they have been hired. Their names are then entered on a database which is distributed to all first-, second-, and third-year teachers.

The remaining two hours of the session are a celebration and a portfolio "show-and-tell." The teacher candidates, grouped according to certification, are seated at tables in the college's Field House. Each student is responsible for a professional appearance, a market-ready portfolio, and a resume ready for distribution. As school personnel from nearby districts arrive, they informally chat with the students while perusing their portfolios. Since these individuals are responsible for hiring, we believe they will be pleased to participate in this event which affords them an early look at potential new teachers.

Portfolio Presentation III will be piloted in the fall semester of 1997. Faculty, teacher candidates, and district personnel eagerly anticipate this final phase of the portfolio process. We expect that the day's activities will be rather bittersweet, since this is a time of both endings and beginnings. As members of the professional community view the portfolios of our teacher candidates, we will recall the personal and professional journeys we have taken with these students. We know that along the way, each version of their portfolios captured their unique stories as they progressed through the program.

CONCLUSION

It is vital that the people working to design the portfolio process believe passionately in what it will do for the students and, ultimately, the teacher preparation program. It is also essential that this group of individuals has a clear and common perception of the process's intended outcome and its relationship to the mission of the teacher preparation program. An agreed-upon methodology should guide the formulation of the portfolio process. Implementation should occur in stages, with each section being piloted and refined before the next stage is begun. Be warned: The planning and implementing is time-consuming and will take several years. We would advise that the same group of people develop the program in its entirety for continuity and consistency of standards.

One of our joys has been recognizing candidates who have compiled exemplary portfolios. At the end of each semester, facilitators recommend that a handful of students from Portfolio I and II participate in table presentations. This experience is an opportunity for faculty and administration to reward and recognize the accomplishments of these students, while providing models for students who have not yet gone through the process.

We feel very strongly that our purpose in developing the portfolio process has been met. Our students have a new awareness of and appreciation for our program's knowledge base and how it translates into authentic practices. The candidates are able to provide evidence of their continued growth and development throughout their educational program.

Just as the candidates' portfolios evolve, so does the portfolio process. Are there ways we can streamline the process without sacrificing its integrity? Must portfolios be presented in hard-copy format or may candidates utilize Hyperstudio or other multimedia? Are there particular formats that hiring personnel in the field prefer? As questions arise, we need to address them and revise the affected criteria.

Despite whatever minor issues may arise, the portfolio process is supported by the strong underpinnings of the knowledge base, the commitment of faculty, and the growing evidence that it really works! The portfolio process has provided a dynamic vehicle for both reflection and documentation. It is our hope that this is only the beginning. We envision that our graduates will continue to set new goals and expectations for themselves and will utilize their portfolios to capture their professionalism.

GLOSSARY

CSC Cardinal Stritch College

DMS Decision Making Seminar: title for the original screening process for admittance to the Advanced Professional Sequence

DPI Department of Public Instruction: state bureau governing teacher education programs and licensing

ED/SEd Education/Special Education: title assigned to the undergraduate teacher education program and its course descriptions

EPRT English Proficiency Requirement Test: a reading/writing test required for graduation from Cardinal Stritch College

FYI First Year Initiative: a mentoring program for first- through third-year beginning teachers from Cardinal Stritch College

GPA Grade Point Average

PBC Post Baccalaureate Certification: certification program designed for students holding an undergraduate degree

PPST Praxis Series/Pre-professional Skills Test: a reading/writing/math test required for certification in the state of Wisconsin

TEC Teacher Education Committee: an all-college decision-making, governing body for the initial certification program
TED Teacher Education Division: title for the college of teacher education at Cardinal Stritch College

REFERENCES

Good, T. L., & Brophy, J. E. (1994). *Looking in classrooms.* New York: Harper Collins Publishers, Inc.

Graeven-Peter, M., & Du Mez, J. (1997). Collaborative networking and teacher induction programs: Creating caring systems of support. *The Delta Kappa Bulletin,* 63(3) 18–21.

Impey, W. D., & McHaney, J. H. (1993). *Reflective inquiry portfolios: A design for development and assessment of teaching and supervision skills.* New Orleans, LA: Mid-South Educational Association. (ERIC Document Reproduction Service No. 367 612)

Murray, F. B. (1996). *The teacher educator's handbook: Building a knowledge base for the preparation of teachers.* San Francisco: Jossey-Bass Publishers.

Nettles, D. H., & Petrick, P. B. (1995). *Fast back 379: Portfolio development for preservice teachers.* Bloomington, IN: Phi Delta Kappa Educational Foundation.

Raines, P., & Shadiow, L. (1996). Reflection and teaching: The challenge of thinking beyond the doing. In F. Schultz (Ed.), *Education 96/97* (pp. 218–221). Guilford, CT: Dushkin Publishing Group.

Ryan, J. M., & Kuhs, T. M. (1993). Assessments of preservice teachers and the use of portfolios. *Theory into Practice,* 32, 75–81.

Synder, J. (1993). *Beyond assessment: University/school collaboration in portfolio review and the challenge to program improvement.* Michigan: Wayne State University. (ERIC Document Reproduction Service No. ED 359 158)

Stanfield, R. L. (1996). Rebel with a cause. In F. Schultz (Ed.), *Education 96/97* (pp. 64–67). Guilford, CT: Dushkin Publishing Group.

Touzel, T. J. (1993). *Portfolio analysis: Window of competence.* Paper presented at the Annual Meeting of the American Association of Colleges for Teacher Education, San Diego, CA. (ERIC Documentation Reproduction Service No. ED 356 207)

ABOUT THE AUTHORS

Joanne A. Anderson has a doctorate in Early and Middle Childhood Studies and has been the Chair of the Initial Certification Program at Cardinal Stritch College in Milwaukee, Wisconsin, for six years. Her interests are in developmentally appropriate practices, classroom management, and teacher preparation programs. She is particularly interested in assessing the dispositions of teacher candidates in teacher preparation programs. In 1993–1994 Dr. Anderson was bestowed the Educator of the Year award by the students of the college. She is actively involved in writing an elementary health curriculum that deals with childhood cancer and the concepts of compassion and empathy versus sympathy. She also has taught with the U.S. Department of Defense in Bankok.

Judith Du Mez is an assistant professor and the Director of Student Teaching at Cardinal Stritch College. Her primary teaching responsibility is within the Initial Certification Program–Elementary Education. She received her undergraduate degree from St. Olaf College in Northfield, Minnesota, and her master's degree from the University of Wisconsin–Madison. She is involved in mentoring/peer coaching, curriculum integration, and Professional Development Schools.

Marian Graeven Peter is an assistant professor in the Initial Certification Department at Cardinal Stritch College. She taught public school (grades K–12) for 12 years, focusing in the area of Early Childhood: Exceptional Education Needs. She now teaches undergraduate and graduate classes in instructional methods and classroom techniques and supervises clinical and student teachers. She received her doctorate degree in Higher Education from Nova Southeastern University in Ft. Lauderdale, Florida. She is an active member of Delta Kappa Gamma Society International, serving as Secretary of the Sigma Chapter and Chair of the Legislative Committee. She is also the organization's Chair of the Wisconsin State Research Committee.

The Power, Production, and Promise of Portfolios for Novice and Seasoned Teachers

The Power, Production, and Promise of Portfolios for Novice and Seasoned Teachers

Alyce Hunter

INTRODUCTION

What do we know and what do we want to know about teacher portfolios?

The use of both process and presentation portfolios to assess student progress and achievement is by no means a new method of evaluating ability and learning. For generations, hopeful art students have trotted off to college interviews with examples that they have collected and selected as their best works. Teachers, school districts, and even entire states, such as Michigan and Vermont, have embraced the notion that portfolios provide a more complete, authentic, and accurate view of what and how a student has learned. Administrators and teachers are just beginning to realize that the development of professional portfolios has the potential to improve teacher performance and to promote professional growth by providing educators with opportunities for self-reflection and collaboration.

THE POWER OF PORTFOLIOS

Why do teachers and administrators use teacher portfolios?

Teachers and administrators choose to initiate and implement professional portfolios, for several distinct yet interconnected reasons:

1. Portfolios provide an assessment option to use in addition to or in place of more traditional teacher evaluation procedures.

2. By creating their own portfolios, teachers model the process for their students,

3. As they gather and select artifacts, teachers become researchers as they analyze and question their own practices,

4. Portfolio development establishes a collaborative relationship between the administrator, the teachers, and others,

5. Portfolio development empowers teachers to express for themselves and the administration who they are and what they believe about teaching in general and their own teaching in particular,

6. The production of teacher portfolios helps experienced teachers relate to preservice teachers who have produced portfolios of their own, and

7. Portfolios can be used as part of a candidate's application for certification by the National Board for Professional Teaching Standards.

Assessing

The teacher portfolio is an important assessment option because it can add breadth and depth to more traditional evaluation procedures such as "surprise" class observations and more detailed clinical supervision experiences. In these techniques, to varying degrees, the administrator's and teacher's comments and interactions are confined to a single class period, teaching strategies, and/or weaknesses. These observations and conferences do not give as complete a picture of the teacher's beliefs and practices as a portfolio.

Portfolios allow the teacher to deliberately "show-off" specific accomplishments. Videotaped lessons, written lesson plans, and student works can be collected and selected at any time. After a wonderful class, teachers no longer have to lament, "Why wasn't my supervisor here to see this one?" because they can now include artifacts from this experience in their portfolio to share with their evaluator. Particularly, superior teachers can benefit from the portfolio assessment option. These exemplars are frequently ignored or given less attention by their assessors because they are not a problem. It is the "squeaky wheel" troubled teacher who typically needs the advice, counsel, and limited time of the administrator. Superior teachers' portfolios allow them to display the whys and whats of their successes for themselves and their administrator.

Modeling

Modeling involves educators actually using the procedures that they require of students and setting an example for the learners regarding how to accomplish a task. Creating a professional portfolio aligns teacher evaluation practices with current trends in student assessment. Many experienced teachers have never themselves been required to produce a portfolio in which they collect, select, and reflect upon their work. Yet these same well-intended professionals know that this process promotes student learning, so they often require learners to produce a portfolio.

The development of a teacher portfolio helps the educator understand and empathize with the students. For example, a fairly common portfolio practice is for teachers to ask students to set general and specific goals for their learning and then to select assignments that reflect progress toward or accomplishment of these goals. When teachers decide to develop portfolios, they often realize that it can be an arduous task to determine one's goals, because such goal-setting makes them decide what they truly value as teachers and then requires them to assemble artifacts to support their beliefs and goals.

The production of a professional portfolio requires that teachers exhibit the same behaviors and learning patterns that they expect from students. Teachers are required to make choices, experiment, and take risks. Such replication by the teacher of tasks assigned to students gives the educator added insight into the process and its achievement. Therefore, the development of a professional portfolio can increase teachers' appreciation of student effort and achievement.

Questioning

As teachers collect, select, reflect, and model, they are, in essence, asking fundamental questions about who they are, what they are teaching, and why they are doing what they are doing. As they compile their portfolios, teachers are really acting as researchers. Through goal-setting, they identify aspects of their classroom and/or school environment to study. Next, they gather and select artifacts and data, then they analyze and reflect upon the materials for selection in their portfolio. Such analysis and reflection can be used to alter and refine future instruction and enhance student learning. Teacher portfolios provide an exciting opportunity for those immersed in the "field"—teachers and administrators—to ask questions and to find answers about what really works in classrooms and in schools.

Collaborating, Cooperating, and Coaching

The development of portfolios establishes a collaborative relationship between the administrator, the teachers, and others. The process and product also encourage practitioners to reflect on both their own individual expectations and institutional expectations and the relationship between them. The process and product also encourage practitioners to talk to each other about a wide range of ideas and ideals from the philosophical to the practical including what are one's beliefs, what is one's philosophy of education, what to include or not to include in a portfolio, and how does one manage the array of artifacts.

Individual teachers and administrators who collaborate to produce portfolios come to view teacher evaluation and assessment not just as the responsibility of the administrator, but as a shared responsibility that will benefit students. For the administrator, promoting this collaboration is most appropriate and practical. As administrators in today's cost-conscious society are assigned more and more roles and duties, they have less and less time and energy to devote to teacher assessment and evaluation. It is essential that today's administrators find practical ways to make their own workload manageable and also to make their employees know that they are valued and valuable. The initiation and implementation of teacher portfolios provides a solution: This process provides a common ground for collaboration and collegiality between administrator and teacher. The process is characterized by traits identified by Sergiovanni (1990), that enhance collegiality and intrinsic motivation. Administrator and teacher cooperate and share their beliefs and practices in an environment of mutual respect. When administrators and teachers help each other, work together, and learn from each other, an atmosphere of trust and professionalism results.

The development of a teacher portfolio and the subsequent relationship between educators is most compatible with the elements of cognitive coaching outlined by Costa and Garmston (1994). Cognitive coaching and portfolio production both acknowledge that teaching is a professional act. The administrator serves as a coach who helps and supports the teacher in the development of the portfolio. Also teachers can act as coaches for each other in this process. They can answer each other's questions about the mundane— "What kind of binder do you use to save your stuff?" and about the sublime—"Do you really believe that all children can learn? How do you know?" The production of professional portfolios involves all participants in discovery learning. Teachers are challenged to question themselves and their practices and encouraged to collaborate with peers and administrators in order to discover better ways to teach and learn.

Empowering the Producer

Not only does the development of teacher portfolios promote collaboration and collegiality, but it also empowers the portfolio developers—the teachers. The teachers feel, believe, and know that they have actual, real, multifaceted input into their own evaluations. The administrator does not have power "over" them. The teachers collect, select, and reflect upon what is important to them. The teachers have the power "to" use their portfolios to gain a new perspective on their teaching, to promote self-assessment and reflection, to support their inquiry into effective practice, and to enhance student learning and their own professional growth.

Linking Teachers with Preservice Educators

The production of teacher portfolios by practicing teachers links experienced teachers to preservice teachers and to the current, fledgling trend for national teacher certification. As outlined in earlier parts of this text, many colleges and universities are suggesting or requiring that preservice teachers develop portfolios to catalog and showcase their abilities and achievements and to present themselves to potential employers. Teaching staffs can "learn new tricks" by examining the contents of these preservice portfolios. They can be challenged to keep up with the neophytes by developing complete and comprehensive portfolios that reflect who and what they are as teachers and professionals.

Portfolios in the National Certification Process

The National Board for Professional Teaching Standards identifies the production of a portfolio as essential. For example, the Early Adolescent/ English Language Arts certification requires that candidates present a portfolio in which they prepare and analyze videotapes of whole-class and small-group instruction, select and analyze student writing and student response to literature, and describe and document professional accomplishments. Additionally, the production of a professional portfolio enforces policy goals of the National Board because it helps teachers think systematically about their actions, helps them learn from their teaching, and encourages them to be active members of the teaching/learning community.

THE PRODUCTION OF PORTFOLIOS
BY NOVICE AND SEASONED TEACHERS

How do administrators and teachers use teacher portfolios?

It is common educational jargon to describe student portfolios as the intersection of instruction and evaluation. In everyday language, this means that portfolios, whether they be those of students or teachers, contain a variety of materials or artifacts for a multitude of reasons. Some of these materials are finished pieces, others are works in progress. Some of these items will be retained for a "best" portfolio, some will be discarded. What all of the items have in common is that they help instruct the users about their own abilities and help them evaluate themselves. Each portfolio is different because it reflects the uniqueness of its creator. Perhaps it is easier to think of portfolios, particularly those generated by teachers, as both a process and a product.

The Process of Collection

Teacher portfolios as a process include the collection, selection, and reflection upon artifacts that tell who the teacher is, what he/she believes is important, and what he/she actually does in the classroom. There is no set rule about what is or is not an artifact. It is up to the discretion of the individual teacher to determine whether an item is appropriate. Artifacts can include items such as the teacher's philosophy of education, graded student work, handouts distributed to students, copies of rubrics or grading scales, notes for teaching, copies of useful articles, bibliographies, bulletin board plans, favorite lessons, publishers' addresses, snapshots, videotapes of lessons, personal critiques of lessons, peer critiques of lessons, minutes of meetings, summaries of team and department activities, parent responses, responses to parents, books read by students, written belief statements about teaching and life, lists of things and practices to keep and to change, reports from conferences, wish lists, "atta boy/girl" notes from administrators, parents, and students, and personal reflections. The list goes on and on.

One teacher advises another who wants to begin the teacher portfolio process: "Start collecting from Day 1. Set aside a period of time each week (or at the end of each unit or project) to gather copies of handouts and samples of students products. Start a notebook right away! This will eliminate a 'portfolio stuff drawer' that never really gets organized." Another teacher suggests that portfolio producers label collected materials with information such as how the artifact might fit into the portfolio. She also cautions that if one assembles video tapes, it is meaningful to attach a written explanation to the tape. For example, if the tape is of a lesson, the written label should identify objectives of the lesson, information about specific students, and/or the participant's judgment of the effectiveness of the instruction.

Wolf (1996) suggested that a convenient way to manage one's portfolio is to have a table of contents that lists three distinct organizational sections: Background information, teaching artifacts and reflections, and professional information. Background information could include a resume, educational philosophy, and goals. The teaching artifacts could contain sample lessons and units and student work. Professional information could include lists of professional activities as well as formal evaluations.

However one chooses to manage the collection of artifacts, it is essential that the collection be cataloged so that it can be shared with one's supervisor. One teacher advises, "Get yourself a sturdy three-ring binder with dividers. Use dividers for major units of study that you cover in your classroom every year. Focus on what you do in the classroom. Don't try to save everything related to teaching such as interesting articles, materials from professional conferences, and other related professional handouts. If you do, you'll need a Mack truck, not a three-ring binder to hold your portfolio!" To make the collection more manageable, an administrator set up parameters for professional portfolios to include required items such as a table of contents, a philosophy of education, and a reflective writing piece in which teachers described their artifact choices and the arrangement of their portfolio. The administrator examined and discussed only these required items, even though some teachers had gathered copious teaching and professional artifacts!

The Process of Selection

Even after artifacts have been collected, the teacher must select items to be maintained in the process portfolio that also could be included in a "best" or presentation portfolio. Selection can be based on the divisions of instruction such as units, skills, or themes. Organization around divisions of instruction is considered most practical by teachers in their first year of portfolio production. Selecting items such as worksheets, student samples, and lesson plans, as one is or has just finished doing and using them is an efficient use of the teacher's time. Immediate collection and selection based upon what one is teaching currently and the organization of these items into predetermined units or curricular categories makes sense to busy teachers, because it does not require additional time to generate and organize new categories.

Using unit or curricular categories is an expedient and practical way to develop a professional portfolio. As one teacher notes, "Make the portfolio practical. It should help you improve instructional materials and ultimately perfect your craft." Another teacher who organizes her portfolio according to instructional units states, "My portfolio is much more valuable than a traditional plan book. The development of a portfolio has helped me to gather my ever-growing array of materials into one notebook, with some organization. It is now easier to 'see' what I am doing at a glance, rather than rummaging through file folders!"

Basis for Selection of Artifacts

Selecting materials to include in the portfolio also can be based on an organizational pattern such as the one suggested by Wolf (1996). Wolf's scheme expanded the idea of collecting artifacts primarily related to teaching and the act of teaching to include biographical information and professional resources that reflect who the educator is as a professional.

Selection of artifacts also can be based on what a teacher believes is important about teaching and learning and students. One practitioner begins her portfolio with a two-page philosophy of education in which she ruminates about her nineteen years of classroom experience. She chooses to highlight four general principles that she believes have guided her over time. She writes, "First of all I believe that good teachers must be active learners . . . Second, I believe that all children can be motivated to work and learn to much higher standards than commonly expected. . . . Third, I believe that the challenge is . . . to help students become successful learners . . . Fourth, teaching also involves building and maintaining partnerships among children, teachers, and parents."

The four beliefs identified by this teacher can be used to glean artifacts. For example, to support the statement that all children can be motivated to work and to learn, the teacher can include samples of ways she has tailored lessons and assignments to meet the needs of and yet challenge immigrant children. To reinforce her belief about maintaining partnerships among children, teachers, and parents, the teacher can include a videotape of a parent–student–teacher conference.

Another practitioner begins her portfolio with a one paragraph statement of educational philosophy in which she describes her belief about her job as a middle-level educator: "I see myself as an expert in my field, a role model, a cheerleader, a confidant, a guardian, a supporter, and a mentor". These seven aspects or roles of a middle-level educator can be used to organize this teacher's portfolio selection. For example, she can document that as a mentor, she participated in the district's Youth Teaching Youth Program. Through this program, high school students return to the middle school to work with a teacher that they admire. This teacher's portfolio can include letters from high school students who have requested to work with her and her students, as well as the middle schoolers' written responses to this experience.

Another teacher specifically concentrates on defining her educational philosophy in relation to the course that she teaches: "I believe that multicultural knowledge has become a critical life skill . . . It is my goal that, through the study of work cultures, my students will resemble seasoned world travelers . . . They will be at ease with differences, understanding their causes and appreciating their effects." One would expect this portfolio to be replete with lesson and unit plans that require learners to think critically about and relate personally to the histories, traditions, and beliefs of numerous cultures.

Selection Based on Individual Goals

Selection also can be dependent upon the goals that teachers have identified for the portfolio and for their teaching. For example, in some states, notably New Jersey, teachers are required to develop Professional Improvement Plans (PIPS) each year. These plans require that professionals set objectives, record activities, and determine methods of assessing goal achievement. A teacher portfolio can be developed to substantiate the completion of a Professional

Improvement Plan. One teacher selected for inclusion those lessons, units, and student work samples that proved he was aligning his instruction with the New Jersey State Core Content Standards for Social Studies. The teacher had designated the alignment of district curriculum and instruction with the State Standards as a Professional Improvement Plan, and his portfolio documented his achievement of this PIP.

Another way for teachers to decide which items to retain in their progress portfolio for possible inclusion in their presentation portfolio is to reflect on their own reasons or purposes for developing the portfolio. Is it to showcase what and how they teach? If this is the reason, then the portfolio should contain items such as sample lesson plans and assessment techniques. Is it to help improve student learning? If this is the reason, then the portfolio should contain samples of student work and reflection. If the purpose of the portfolio collection and selection is for a combination reasons, the artifacts should demonstrate compliance with these reasons.

A most optimistic practitioner believes, "I would also suggest that they become very clear on the purpose for the portfolio before they begin. I think that the portfolio will naturally become what it needs to be but starting with a direction will help." As one "portfolio rookie" stated, "Determine what it is that this portfolio will do for you or what you want it to do for you. This effort to determine your purpose is very time consuming and can become frustrating at times!"

Another participant lamented that the hardest part of the process was to determine the portfolio's purpose and identify objectives and artifacts that demonstrate this purpose. However, she also commented that the difficulty she experienced with identifying her personal purpose and objectives has increased her understanding of this purpose/ objective process. She believes that this new understanding had enhanced and refined her classroom planning and teaching.

Dating Artifacts to Show Growth

Whether portfolio practitioners choose to organize their collection and selection of materials based on instructional units, educational philosophy, or personal goals, it is helpful for practitioners to consider the various ways that the contents of these categories can or should be organized. Three strategies include: (a) organization by chronological order, (b) organization by successes, and (c) organization by hypertext.

Chronological order is the most common form of organizing materials in a professional portfolio. This method of ordering the artifacts and reflections by date implicity shows change, growth, and/or completion of a portfolio objective.

Portfolio developers also can choose to organize their efforts by successes to demonstrate growth from "weak to better to best." This type of organization usually, but not always, mirrors chronological organization. For example, teachers might choose to include in their portfolios instances or artifacts that demonstrate that they are trying to increase their teaching repertoire by including a new strategy or technique. Initially the students might respond well to the change. However, they eventually might tire of this new strategy and respond better to techniques with which they are more familiar. The students also might need additional practice with the new technique so that they can become more adept at using it. Thus, the teacher's evidence of personal as well as student change and growth might be organized by successes that are not necessarily in chronological order. Some teachers like to reverse the "weak to best" order to "best to weak." By doing so, they display the positive, ultimate success of work as the first impression in the portfolio rather than starting with one's foibles as the first impression.

Portfolio producers who use a computer disk as a portfolio or who add computer-generated materials to their more traditional portfolios might find it interesting and challenging to organize their entries by hypertext. Hypertext allows users to create graphics and to use visuals, sounds, and movement in order to organize and enhance text.

Some portfolio producers caution that it is possible to become "obsessed" or "bogged down" by these organizational strategies and decisions. To avoid this they suggest that potential participants who are not able to decide on a specific organizational strategy should proceed by collecting and selecting a scope of artifacts without a predetermined strategy. This advice suggests that the neophyte choices will point to an organizational pattern. A teacher who has produced professional portfolios for three consecutive years further comments that organizational structures might change over the years or even during one year.

Challenges of Organization and Selection of Artifacts

However portfolio developers choose to organize their collection and selection of materials, this part of the portfolio process challenges them to think about the whats, whys, and hows of their teaching. The selection part of the process requires that they ask themselves essential questions about their teaching practice and choose artifacts to answer these questions. "Being selective does not mean constructing a biased picture of one's teaching performance but rather a fair and generous representation of it." (Zubizarreta, 1994). Selection requires teachers to use the higher-order thinking skills of analysis, synthesis, and evaluation.

As one portfolio veteran notes, "Prior to a new unit of study, I now review the teaching artifacts I collected from the last year. These artifacts include items such as assignment sheets, process sheets, student samples, student comments and evaluations, and ways of assessing the unit. I spend time reviewing and revising my plans, and when needed, adding new material and assignments. The result seems to be more 'polished pieces' of classroom lessons. This is reflected in the student samples and new assessment tools, specifically the development of rubrics. The portfolio has made it possible to reflect upon what I have done in the past and improve upon it."

The Process of Reflection

However, if the teachers' participation in the portfolio process is to be most beneficial to themselves and to their students, it must go beyond selection and haphazard rumination to include formalized methods of reflection and self-evaluation. While it is true that the self-selection of artifacts by the portfolio practitioner is by its very nature a subtle form of reflection and evaluation, the formalization of reflective procedures adds the metacognitive component to the process.

In other words, teachers are challenged to be cognizant of their goals, beliefs, and actions and to reflect upon these goals, beliefs, and actions. Furthermore, they are called upon to use these reflections to select ways to enhance and improve their teaching. A teacher comments, "As I continue with the selection/reflection phases, I can hopefully evaluate more deeply and weed out and improve lessons and projects." Reflection is the act of taking the time to step back and away—to look at oneself as a teacher and as a person. It is the part of the professional portfolio process that helps the teacher be conscious and responsible and that helps the teacher see and realize what he/she does and who he/she is.

Categorizing and Formalizing Personnel Reflection

There are various ways to categorize and formalize the personal reflective process. Reflection can be organized by time—that is, when the portfolio developer chooses to comment. Some believe that the end of a unit, or teaching experience is the most appropriate time. "At the end of the unit, if you notice something that worked well, write it down on the artifact. For example, if you believe that more time was needed on a part of the project, make note of that insight. Your personal notes and reflections are a wonderful instructional resource the following year." Others consider it essential "to try for self reflection at the end of every day and then work up to after every class period." One practitioner records his responses for each day in his traditional teacher plan book and later transfers appropriate reflections to his portfolio. Not only do his daily reflections serve to reinforce his portfolio's purpose, but also he now has a priceless personal diary of his last three years of teaching!

In addition to, or in place of, the formative evaluative strategies of unit conclusion or daily reflections, some teachers choose, at the end of each year, to write a narrative commenting on the process and their portfolio's contents. Zubizarreta (1994) suggested that the process of writing a summation narrative that concisely organizes details of teaching efforts and accomplishments is critical to the portfolio participants. He even states that the ideal length for such written documentation is between eight and ten double-spaced pages.

Whatever length reflection a participants choose, writing a summative evaluation allows them to consider the entire body of artifacts as evidence to support their portfolio's purpose and goals and their own educational philosophy. It also permits practitioners to reflect upon whether the time and energy they devoted to the producing the portfolio were worthwhile. After completing her first attempt at portfolio development, one teacher writes, "The time requirement is large, but so are the benefits." It helps a teacher to crystallize his/her thinking, to become a truly reflective teacher. Similarly after her first year of portfolio selection and collection, another practitioner ruminates, "Developing a teacher portfolio has helped me a great deal. It has given my daily lessons more structure, allowed me to make helpful comments on what worked and what didn't work, and how I can adapt, change or improve the units and lessons for the following year. It also promoted self-discipline."

Organizing a Portfolio Cycle

Another example of a technique to organize self-reflection according to a time parameter is to organize the entire portfolio process into a cycle. This cycle can be based on models that teachers already employ in their classrooms with their students. One such model is the writing-process cycle. Students are taught that writing is a recursive process that involves prewriting drafting, revising, rewriting, and publishing.

Likewise, teachers who develop professional portfolios can relate the writing-process cycle model to their portfolio production. For example, as they compile their portfolios, they can use such prewriting strategies as brainstorming and graphic organizers to determine their purpose. They can consider the collection stage as similar to the drafting stage of writing because both involve the gathering of relevant information. Teachers also can consider that the revising and rewriting stages of the writing process are similar to what they do as they collect and reflect upon their teaching artifacts. The presentation portfolio can be likened to the publishing stage of writing because just as writers finalize text to share with their audience, so the producers of portfolios analyze and presents their work for themselves and their peer or supervisory audiences. Finally by using the writing-process cycle model to organize their portfolio process, professionals can come to realize that both processes are truly recursive—bending backward, never-ending ways to analyze their efforts. As one teacher says, "... this is a long-term process, not a 'rush' project."

The Student Portfolio as a Model for the Professional Portfolio

In addition to considering the writing process as a cycle model for portfolio initiation and implementation, teachers can adopt and adapt the strategies that they or other professionals have developed to manage and to set time lines for student portfolio accomplishments to the process and product of teacher portfolios. For example, typical student portfolio cycles involve setting goals, determining appropriate deadlines (weekly, monthly, or end of marking period) for selecting and collecting of samples and self-reflecting about these artifacts, conferencing with peers and teacher, and presenting the final product portfolio.

Teachers can adapt these cycles to develop a time line for their portfolios. An example of such an adaptation with specific deadlines is: (a) set goals—completed previous year, (b) collect artifacts—weekly—be sure to include lesson plans, assessment instruments, and student work samples, (c) self-reflect—biweekly—discard artifacts that do not relate to goals, (d) conference with peers and supervisor—monthly—ask advice about inclusions, and (e) prepare and present portfolio—yearly—be sure to select, collect, and reflect on the "best" piece to meet each goal.

Strategies to Promote Self-Reflection

While it is essential to organize one's time in relation to the self-reflection segment of the portfolio process, practitioners also need to consider how or what specific strategies to use to promote this self-reflection and evaluation. Many teachers are used to more traditional forms of supervision such as classroom observation followed by a teacher/supervisor conference. In this model, it is the supervisor's responsibility to observe and record descriptions of what he/she sees and to comment upon whether he/she values or likes what he/she sees going on in the classroom.

The reflective portion of the professional portfolio process requires teachers not to depend solely on their supervisor's viewpoint, but rather to discover and acknowledge what they themselves see and value in their teaching. Just as students who produce portfolios must be trained in the unaccustomed practice of self-reflection (Camp 1992), teachers must learn strategies and techniques to facilitate this part of the portfolio process.

Teachers who have little or no experience with self-reflection might adapt the strategy of taking inventory of their perceptions of themselves (Camp 1992). Such fledgling teachers could ask themselves a series of questions such as: "What do I like most about my teaching?", "What do I like least about my teaching?", "What do I think is important for others to know about me as a teacher?". They can answer these questions either orally to others or written for themselves or to share with other teachers or their supervisor. The specific answers or the specific questions are not as important as the fact that teachers are challenging themselves to think about what they do and who they are. Additionally, they are challenging themselves to think about and internalize a process for self-reflection.

While thinking about and critiquing their own work is not alien to most teachers, many have had little or no opportunity or experience with formalized ways to develop skills related to metacognition and self-evaluation. Again, teachers can look to strategies that they use with their students to help them develop these self-reflective skills.

The use of reflection prompts is a fairly common strategy in classrooms that use process learning and portfolio assessment. These prompts can be adapted by teachers for their own use in the professional portfolio process. Appropriate prompts and questions include those that require the participant to think not only about specific artifacts, but also to consider the entire process of collection, selection, and reflection. Examples or prompts and questions are: I have chosen to organize my portfolio by . . . because . . . , I have chosen to include this piece in my portfolio because . . . , If I had a chance to do this activity again, I would . . . because . . . , What was the best thing about keeping a portfolio?, What was the worst thing about keeping a portfolio?, and What advice would you give to someone who wants to begin the portfolio process?

Teachers who have produced professional portfolios also have learned that the selection or "weeding" aspect of the process is an important form of reflection. This selection forces them to reflect upon why they include certain artifacts and exclude others. Practitioners have found that it is expedient as well as useful to write down their reactions during the selection process.

Conferencing with Peers

Another process that promotes and enhances self-reflection that teachers frequently use with students is peer conferencing. Peer conferencing involves consulting with equals about one's work. The peers, who are involved in the same or a similar assignments or projects, are able and willing to provide appropriate feedback not only because they themselves have the experience of working on similar tasks, but also because they can benefit from the reciprocal feedback that will be provided. In a process-oriented classroom, instructors frequently encourage such peer interactions. Likewise, teachers, as they develop their professional portfolios, can look to each other as confidants, consultants, and counselors. Such collaboration and cooperation among peers is a non-judgmental interaction that can build trust and has the potential to create a community of educators.

Professional portfolio peer conferencing can be either informally or formally organized. Informally, teachers can ask each other for advice about any part of the process and product. They can do things such as observe each other's classes or look at and comment upon each other 's portfolios. Observation of classes can be as informal as a drop-in visit followed by a generalized or portfolio-specific discussion between teachers. Observation of each other's classes also can be as defined as a participant identifying particular aspects of the lesson that relate to the portfolio project and asking his/her peer to observe and comment specifically on the portfolio connection. Peer commenting upon portfolio contents can be as natural as a casual conversation between friends. Peer commenting also can be as defined as including written comments in each other's portfolios.

Some practitioners have found it most beneficial to formally organize in order to share their ideas relating to materials included and the process used for creation of their portfolios. One group develops an agenda and meets each month. A sample agenda from a preliminary meeting includes: (a) greetings—Why did I choose to create a portfolio?, (b) reporting—What am I doing?, (c) comparing—From today's meeting, what can I incorporate into my portfolio process?, and (d) reflecting—Why am I doing what I am doing (in my classroom, with my students, and in my portfolio content/process)? This group's agenda for a meeting near the end of the school year required them to share their self-reflection in order to enlighten their peers by asking them to respond and discuss the following prompts: Has the development of a teacher portfolio helped your teaching during the past year? and What advice would you give to a teacher who wanted to begin the teacher portfolio process?

Portfolio Partnerships

Another way to formally organize peer interactions for the portfolio process is to have participants pair up as portfolio pairs. These pairs can either select each other or be assigned by an administrator. The pairings could involve considerations such as matching participants with similar portfolio goals, comparing portfolio decisions of two individuals who teach the same grade or subject, and having cross-experience interactions (a seasoned portfolio producer matched with a novice).

The pair's function as partners is to help each other complete the process and product. In replication of the ideas and ideals of cognitive coaching, such partnerships encourage mutual trust and learning. Paradoxically, just as in cognitive coaching situations, participants who have been involved as "pair-share" portfolio pairs have found that the peer relationship has improved their performance as autonomous teachers and portfolio producers and has also helped them to "realize their interdependence with other professionals" (Costa & Garmston, 1994).

Peers should devise formats for evaluative feedback from their colleagues. For example, a portfolio producer who asks a peer to observe a lesson should provide the peer with the purpose of the lesson, the method of instruction, and examples of the specific feedback he/she desires. A written peer-to-peer format facilitates consistent and accurate communication. Other specific exercises, activities, and handouts that elaborate the possible ways to facilitate portfolio partnerships can be found in the professional development facilitator's guide published by Dietz (1993).

Conferencing with Administrators

Just as portfolio participants can gain insight from consulting and working with peers, conferencing with an administrator can help teachers with their collection, selection, and reflection. Such conferencing between administrator and teacher can be as informal as a chat in the school hallway or the staff member inviting the administrator to informally observe a class or practice and then discuss reactions. Conferencing between administrator and teacher also can be formalized into routinely scheduled meetings. The purposes, format, and outcomes of these meetings can be modeled on and will be much the same as the conferences that teachers have with students about writing, reading, and learning.

Professional portfolio conferences provide a venue for the administrator to find out what teachers believe, how they think and organize, what they find exciting, and how they feel about various educational topics and learning theories. Such conferences also give both the administrator and the teacher the chance to cooperatively and collaboratively develop mutual language and a framework for professional development.

The advice about student–teacher portfolio conferences and teacher feedback given by Farr and Trumbull (1997) in *Assessment Alternatives for Diverse Classrooms* can be adapted to make it applicable to teacher–administrator meetings. Through conferencing, teachers can work with administrators to continue to develop an understanding of the purpose and power of professional portfolios and to enhance knowledge about the processes of collection, selection, and reflection. Teachers and administrators can use "the common ground" of the conference to talk about personal challenges and how they feel about the work and the profession of teaching.

An atmosphere of trust and shared responsibility can be the outcome of such conferencing. Moreover, the entire professional portfolio process has the potential to deepen the trust and relationship between administrators and teachers because both parties have taken the risk to expose what they believe and to acknowledge the impact they have on each other. Such mutual risk-taking is based on the belief and assumption that each individual has integrity and is sensitive to the needs of the other (Kouzes & Posner, 1987). However, administrators are cautioned to remember that their role is most often not just one of collaboration but also one of evaluation. Therefore, some teachers might be reluctant to share situations in which they took a teaching risk that was not successful or even to set portfolio goals that they will have to work hard to achieve and document.

Advice to Administrators

Conferencing between administrator and teacher has the potential to reveal both positive and negative aspects of teacher performance that are not always evident in a classroom. Through one-on-one conversations with teachers, an administrator has the chance to ask important questions and have meaningful dialogues about practices such as why an individual chooses to use a certain instructional strategy or how a teacher adapts instruction for learning styles or different intelligences.

These conversations also can reveal that the collaborators have distinctly different educational philosophies. For example, trust and free conversations can reveal that an administrator and a teacher disagree as to whether instruction should be primarily child-centered or content-driven. To maintain a collaborative relationship, in such instances, both parties must agree either to work to generate a consensus opinion or to disagree politely in order to continue working toward the common good of effective teaching. Ideally, the administrator and the teacher can search together for integrative answers that change the emphasis of each other's thinking from the either/or dichotomy to an emphasis on reciprocal goals and processes.

It is important for the administrator to remember that teachers can be overwhelmed with too many questions or too much input. Too much advice, no matter how well intended, can leave teachers feeling inadequate and insecure not only with the professional portfolio process, but also with their teaching. It is best for an administrator at the beginning of the conferencing procedure to keep things simple and positive. An initial conference conversation might be confined to discussing something that the teacher feels he/she is doing well and would like to include in their portfolio. However, it must never be forgotten that if teachers and administrators are to be collaborators in the conferencing process, it is permissible and appropriate for teachers to initiate the conference and direct the course of the discussion.

Defining the Teaching Versus the Teacher Portfolio

The administrator's role in the conferencing process and in the entire professional portfolio production must also be determined and directed by the type of professional portfolio the participant produces. One distinction can be made by defining portfolios as representative of either teaching or the teacher.

A "teaching portfolio" illustrates in its collection, selection, and reflection what is done and accomplished in the classroom. As such, the artifacts would include lessons, units, and assessment techniques with teacher reflections. This type of portfolio is primarily concerned with recording, guiding, and enhancing teaching. A "teacher portfolio," on the other hand, illustrates in its collection, selection, and reflection, the teacher as an instructor, as a professional, and as a person. As such, the artifacts could include not only teaching materials, but also more personal materials such as resumes, educational philosophy, letters of recommendation, formal evaluations, and teachers' comments about articles in professional journals. This type of portfolio attempts to give a more complete view of the teacher as a multifaceted professional compared to the teaching portfolio, which concentrates on the act of teaching and its consequences.

Either type of portfolio is acceptable as long as the producer sets definite goals and uses either type to collect, select, and reflect upon artifacts to realize these goals. Some novice portfolio producers have found that while they began the project with the grandiose idea of producing a document that presented an overall picture of themselves as a professional, the realities of daily teaching and its subsequent time constraints forced them to rethink their goals. One "rookie" cautions, "Stay on top of things—don't let calendars, lessons, or hand-outs pile up for too long!" Another advises, "The advice I would give to a teacher who is going to give this a try is to be realistic about how long it takes to compile and reflect on a huge body of work like a portfolio."

The Portfolio of the "Above-Average" Teacher

The administrator's role in the development of teaching or teacher portfolios is profoundly complicated by the reality that administrators are formally charged with documenting the competency and hence employability of teachers. For "above-average" teachers—those who surpass the districts and/or administrator's performance expectations—the portfolio process, including conferencing with administrators, can provide the added recognition for a "job well-done."

Administrators can use the portfolio process to recognize and praise the teacher's strengths. Such commendation and praise, Blase and Kirby (1992) have concluded, helps instructors to maintain and develop skills, as well as to feel confident and satisfied with their work. In other words, when administrators interact and collaborate on professional portfolios with "above-average" teachers, the attention and positive response of the administrators has the potential to cause these exemplars to perform even better. In addition, administrators, through collaboration with "above-average" teachers on the process of collecting, selecting, and reflecting, can create an accepting environment in which these teachers feel comfortable to be risk-takers and innovators with regard to instructional strategies and curriculum development.

The Portfolio of the "Average" and Marginal Teacher

For "average"—those who do a competent, adequate job in the school district's and/or administrator's assessment—or "marginal"—those who are in danger of not providing adequate and appropriate instruction—teachers, the portfolio process, including conferencing with the administrator, demonstrates the administrator's willingness to help the teacher. Also the development of a professional portfolio gives these teachers the opportunity to display their skills and talents. It gives them the chance to address areas that the administrator has noted as areas of concern or deficiency and to document that they have worked to improve these weaknesses.

In essence, through the portfolio process of collecting, selecting, and reflecting upon their teaching, average or marginal teachers can come to believe and feel that they have worthwhile input into their own evaluation of their performance. Portfolio production provides the opportunity for reconciling their own beliefs and practices with those of critical administrators. It provides the opportunity for recognizing their own ability to improve performance so that their performance coincides more closely with administrative and district expectations.

The teacher-initiated activities that include collecting of, selecting of, and reflecting upon the contents of the portfolio present to the administrator not only the materials that the teacher values, but also the teachers' personal and introspective thoughts. In this way, artifacts provide the administrator with new insight into the teacher and give the administrator and the teacher specific materials on which to focus and collaborate during portfolio conferencing.

This collaboration on what teachers choose to include or not to include in their portfolios is, in a very real sense, a rejection of the old clinical model of teacher assessment of the average or marginal teacher that looks for what is wrong with teaching and writes a prescription to fix it. The teacher-centered nature of the portfolio process demands that participants first look at what teachers consider as strengths. Then participants can work together to identify either why both the administrator and teacher consider these attributes as strengths or why they disagree on the effect of the artifacts selected and reflected upon by the teacher.

The Portfolio of the "Below-Average" Teacher

In order to work effectively with below-average teachers—those whose performance does not meet distrcit's and adminsitrator's expectations and demands—it is helpful and essential that the administrator has collected, selected, and reflected upon the teacher's performance. The administrator should bring to a portfolio conference any written documentation—such as their formal and informal observations of the teacher, information from parents, teaching peers, and other administrators and student test results—that would facilitate intelligent interaction with the portfolio producer. For example, if a teacher contends and provides documentation using a sample of student work, that they have taught a specific skill, a prepared administrator can produce standardized test results to verify or show a discrepancy in the teacher's belief. If there is discrepancy, the teacher and the administrator can begin a professional dialogue about the reasons why the portfolio producer felt as he/she did and what caused students to falter on the standardized measure of achievement.

With "below-average" teachers, the portfolio process takes on the added dimension of whether or not the portfolio is used as an evaluative tool to measure teacher growth or as an evaluative tool that delineates teacher competency or in the case of the below average teacher, incompetency. If one assumes that the portfolio project is a mutually agreed upon endeavor between a teacher and the supervisor, the portfolio should give evidence of the interaction between them as they collaborate to improve the teacher's classroom performance. They could collaborate to identify specific weaknesses that need to be improved and documented. For example, if they agree that the teacher needs to improve communication with parents, then this should be identified as a portfolio objective, and evidence should be gathered by the teacher that provides proof to the supervisor that the teacher is working toward or is in the "process" of improving communication with parents.

Such documentation might include tangibles such as logs of telephone conversations that indicate name of parent contacted, date, subject and length of conversation, and a teacher written summary of the conversation and the subsequent actions of parent, student, and/or teacher. Another tangible that can lead to a collaborative discussion between the teacher and the supervisor is to have the teacher write out what he/she says to parents on Back-to-School Night or Open House. This gives both parties in the portfolio collaboration the chance to consider how this welcoming speech can be interpreted by parents and to refine the teacher's presentation. It gives to the supervisor an opportunity to discuss subtleties of teacher behavior such as tone of voice and demeanor.

Yet another form of documentation would be episodic. In this case, a teacher writes about a specific incident when he/she communicated with a parent. For example, a teacher could record his/her questions and parents' responses during a conference, as well as the teacher's overall impression of the conference. The supervisor and teacher could then meet to discuss the teacher's responses and reactions relating them to the responses and reactions of the parents.

To extend the idea of the collaborative aspect of the professional portfolio to the parent conference, both teacher and supervisor could attend and keep notes on the conference. They would then compare and contrast notes. This could lead to a mutually respectful dialogue about the importance of providing families with information about both the instructional program and their student's achievement, as well as the importance of engaging families in the instructional program.

Of course, the identification by the below-average teacher and the supervisor of mutually acceptable and agreed upon objectives for improvement is "easier said than done." Sometimes, a supervisor can barter with the teacher in order to identify portfolio objectives. The teacher could identify one objective that relates to something that he/she feels he/she does well. The supervisor would counter with a mutually agreed upon objective that targets an area to be improved. Oftentimes, a supervisor must battle with below-average teachers to get them to realize, accept, and internalize that their performance is not what it should be. The supervisor must acknowledge and confront such teachers as adults who are, at best, uncomfortable and, at-worst, defensive or belligerent at being dubbed inadequate or below-average.

This is the time for a supervisor to use his/her best negotiation and conflict-management skills to help the teacher. A basic operational framework for the supervisor would begin with planning the negotiation or confrontation with the teacher. This means the supervisor must be clear on the objective or objectives that he/she and the teacher will work toward as the teacher produces a portfolio. It is the responsibility of the supervisor to provide a suitable climate for meeting with the teacher to inform him/her of what is expected and to answer any questions about expectations. The supervisor should work with the below-average teacher to brainstorm objectives and/or documentation for the portfolio with the goal of mutually choosing objectives and artifacts that display the best of the teacher's performance and ability.

The supervisor must often demonstrate extreme persistence and perseverance as he/she attempts to convince the teacher of the efficiency of a professional portfolio as a means to improve teacher performance or of the viability of the objectives that the supervisor feels are important. Sometimes, teachers are so entrenched in their own defense, their teaching, or both that they refuse to or, at best, half-heartedly participate in the development of a professional portfolio. This is the time for the supervisor to practice leadership by "outrage."

In this extreme method, the supervisor demands that the teacher produce a professional portfolio. It is important for the supervisor to passionately express that this process will help the teacher improve or, at the very least, realize his/her deficiencies. Although authoritative mandating of the production of a portfolio, which has as one of its tenets a collegial and collaborative relationship between supervisor and teacher, might seem or actually be contradictory, this mandate by the supervisor can be seen as the first step toward developing a more collegial and collaborative relationship with the below-average teacher. This mandate puts the teacher "on notice" that the supervisor cares deeply enough about instruction and the students to demand that the teacher improve. The professional portfolio process and product provide the teacher the opportunity to document his/her beliefs and performance. The professional portfolio process and product provide the below-average teacher with the opportunity to prove that what he/she is doing or being is not unsatisfactory.

However, the use of a portfolio is not a panacea for all below-average teachers and the supervisors who work with them. Nor is the mandate to produce a portfolio a guarantee that the teacher will use this tool to analyze and reflect upon his/her deficiencies. It is a tool that can be used to begin a professional dialogue, but it is not foolproof. Through engaging with the below-average teacher in the professional portfolio process, the supervisor will come to a better understanding of who the teacher is and what he/she does.

What happens however, when the supervisor does not like what he/she comes to understand about this teacher? Perhaps there are several possibilities: The supervisor's task will be as simple as identifying that the portfolio process did not help this teacher become better because there was a flaw in the process itself, such as artifacts were collected that did not prove an objective or did not help the teacher improve instruction or performance. The supervisor could decide to continue to use the professional portfolio process and product to work with the teacher but to refine expectations and artifact collection. Perhaps the supervisor's task will be to acknowledge that despite the fact that the teacher fulfilled all the requirements for the portfolio production he/she is still an unsatisfactory teacher. The supervisor could decide to use a different means of demanding and monitoring for improvement such as repeated classroom visits and conferences. Perhaps the supervisor's task will be as difficult as accepting that despite his/her best efforts, including participating in the process and production of a professional portfolio, this below-average teacher is incapable of improvement. In this case, it is an ethical decision, based on the original understanding between the teacher and supervisor, for the supervisor to determine whether the data and artifacts that have been gathered in the portfolio process can or should be used to verify the teachers incompetence and to pursue his/her dismissal.

THE PRESENTATION OF THE PROFESSIONAL PORTFOLIO

The completion of a teacher portfolio, whether it occurs at the end of the school year when all objectives are satisfied or upon the completion of a specific objective during the year, implies that in some way the producer will present his/her work to an audience. The concept of the presentation of the professional portfolio can be considered by answering journalism's five Ws (what, who, where, why) as well as one H (how).

Housing the Portfolio

The first W "what" involves a decision that many participants make at the onset of the project—deciding what type of receptacle will hold their artifacts and reflections. Many opt for a large, divided binder. This type of binder organization helps during the process because teachers, when they are rushed for time, will simply place behind the relevant divider, artifacts that they want to examine later. In this way, the binder conveniently helps to facilitate the collection and selection processes. Other teachers use the binder as a final receptacle for what they have retrieved from their portfolio cabinet file drawer and have selected for reflection. Some teachers use a collection of smaller binders: Each small binder is earmarked for one portfolio objective and subsequent artifacts and reflections. Covers of the binders can be decorated to reflect the portfolio's contents. For example, a social studies teacher's binder proudly displays pictures of her students as active learners in various poses including project presentations and cooperative grouping. These pictures are superimposed upon a map of the world which symbolizes the course curriculum—World Cultures.

In addition to being accessible and manageable, the use of a binder for the professional portfolio offers convenient storage. The binder can be easily placed on a bookshelf or desk. Some teachers who have been involved in professional portfolio production for more than a year, proudly line up their binders on their shelves or desks as a testament of who they are, where they were, and where they are going. Such a line-up not only gives them feelings of accomplishment and pride, but also invites the teachers to reflect upon and compare each year's objectives, artifacts, and reflections.

A problem with the binder system is how to include bulky items such as videotapes. Some practitioners insert pocket portfolios into their binders to hold oversized items. Others use a "see other" type of notation in which they state in their portfolio binder information such as "videotape to demonstrate this objective was made on (date) and is available from the teacher." One teacher uses a treasure chest approach. She stores her portfolio in a large box with a lid. She favors this technique because sometimes the student samples she elects to collect and select are posters or other works of art.

In the spirit of the idea and concepts behind the development of professional portfolios, participants should be allowed to select their own ways to house their portfolios. In reality, some teachers, particularly those new to the process, prefer being given a binder by their supervisor. For these participants, the binder makes the task easier because it helps them to define a limit for collection and selection. The limit and the challenge is to refine the process and product so that it can be contained in one binder! The binder storage method has distinct advantages for the supervisor because the book can be easily brought to teacher/supervisor conferences, can be understood by other teachers and administrators who are not involved in the production, and can be conveniently stored for reference.

Using Technology

The portfolio can also be compiled electronically, with information collected, stored, and reflected upon on a computer disk. A participant could begin by designing and designating files for the contents of the portfolio. For example, files can be categorized and titled in classifications such as philosophy or objectives. Adding items to these files would require the teacher to type each entry in, copy relevant materials from disks of students, peers, and/ or supervisor, or scan artifacts by using a hyperstudio component. The time-line controller or dating mechanism on the computer would make it easy for the producer to remember when he/she processed a particular artifact.

The possibilities for enhancing a professional portfolio that utilizes a computer and is recorded on a disk are endless. A supervisor could create text documents or add text comment to the teacher's work. If the computer were equipped with a microphone, music, speeches, and other performances could be recorded and imported into the portfolio. Through e-mail or an online service, one could even communicate and collaborate with others, including teachers in different schools, who are doing similar projects. Storing the professional portfolio on a computer disk has the advantage of being more compact and transportable than a binder. However, depending upon the type of computer and program used, this type of storage might not be as accessible as a binder unless the producer also produced a hard copy of his/ her portfolio.

While it might seem to some that the decision of what to use to store portfolio items is trite or easy, those who have initiated and implemented professional portfolios realize that it is an important decision. The selection of a receptacle to contain what one values about teaching and why one values what they do, not only defines and limits the task, but also tells a lot about the participant.

Sharing and Displaying the Portfolio

The presentation of the final portfolio, whether it is in the form of a binder, computer disk, or some other container, entails determining to whom, when, where, and why the portfolio will be presented. It is expected that the teacher will display successful completion of the objectives and the project to his/her supervisor. This can be done at a final, end-of-the-school-year, individual conference as well as during the year when an objective is accomplished. Another possible format to use for one-on-one presentation can be adapted from the strategy that Ingalls (1993) describes to assess student writing portfolios. This strategy involves "interviewing" a portfolio by asking and answering questions just as in a job interview. A supervisor could adapt this strategy to a format in which the portfolio producer "becomes" his/her portfolio. As the personified portfolio, the teacher could be asked to respond to prompts such as "tell me who you are" and "tell me why you are important for the teacher and the students."

Sharing with Peers

Teachers who have been involved in the peer aspect of portfolio development often want to share their product with peers who have been helpful. Like the supervisor/teacher interaction, peer interaction can be informal or formal. Some considerations for the peer presentations are logistical such as deciding exactly how long the presentation should be, where the presentation should take place, and when the presentation should happen. Some peers decide to meet and collaborate either quarterly or mid-year so that they can offer each other advice and support as well as congratulations. However, it would seem that the most logical time for the peer presentation would be at the end of the school year in order to allow one's peers to help the individual appreciate his/her accomplishments and to celebrate the completion of the portfolio.

While the end of the year is certainly acceptable and commendable for such celebration, one group of teachers selected the beginning of the next school year as the ideal time for presenting their portfolios. They felt that if they did the presentations at the end of the year, when they were tired and rushed with end-of-the-year events such as graduation, the portfolio sharing would take on the aspect of yet another "ending" activity. While acknowledging that the presentation would be an ideal closure activity for their portfolio projects, these teachers chose to delay the presentation until the start of the next school year.

They made their decision based on the idea that sharing their previous success at the start of the new school year would provide inspiration for themselves and the other participants. In other words, explaining their portfolios and viewing the portfolios of others would give them the impetus and ideas with which to launch their new portfolio projects. So the completed projects not only prompted communal celebration, but also affected how the participants would act and react during the subsequent school year. These participants also felt that the sharing of ideas and accomplishments at the start of the school year was most relevant to their own "mind sets:" Because the practitioners were busy making decisions about their year's portfolio they were most eager and receptive to others' ideas and suggestions.

In addition to the logistical questions of when and where to peer-share finished products, those who have completed their professional portfolios should also consider additional audiences for their sharing presentation. They need to answer critical questions such as what do they want to accomplish with the audience, what do they want the audience to learn about the portfolio producer, and what do they want the audience to learn about the professional portfolio process and product.

Some practitioners answer these questions by deciding that the format for the presentation will be reciprocal: Only those who have developed a portfolio will be present, because only they will understand and be able to effectively comment and evaluate another's process and product. While there is validity to the idea that only through "doing" does one know and appreciate effort, other portfolio producers are more inclusive. They invite teachers and administrators who have not been involved in the process to their presentations. They view these interlopers as the source of constructive criticism and thoughtful questions and as possible converts to the potential and power of professional portfolios.

In addition to deciding who will attend, the participants also need to decide how the presentation will be formatted. Will one person present his/her work while others will be ready with questions or comments? Will all present their portfolios and then comment upon each others?

Peer-sharing presentations can present a dilemma for the supervisor. Should such presentations be voluntary or mandatory? If a supervisor believes that an essential component of the portfolio process is presentation and defense of the finished product, shouldn't it be sufficient to present the documentation to oneself and one's supervisor with attendance at a peer gathering as an option? However, a supervisor knows that it would be a rich communal experience for others to share the teacher's portfolio process and product. In other words, teachers are often the best teachers of teachers. The portfolio producer is not the only one who can or should learn from what he/she does. Perhaps the supervisor should do more than suggest attendance, but should strongly urge or mandate participation for all portfolio producers and all other teachers in these collaborative and cooperative presentations.

Displaying Portfolios for Parents and Students

In addition to presenting finished product portfolios to peers, the portfolios can be displayed to parents and students. One teacher proudly exhibits her work as part of her school's Evening of Excellence production. She believes that displaying her portfolio not only helps parents to realize that a teacher's day is not over at 3 o'clock, but also, more importantly, has the potential to engage parents and teachers in significant dialogue about teaching and learning. Another way to communicate to parents about professional portfolios is for a single participant or a group of portfolio producers to approach their school's parent/teacher organization to decide ways to inform parents. Perhaps a PTA meeting could be devoted to teachers' presentations, or an item could appear in a school newsletter.

In addition to presenting their efforts to parents, teachers might chose to present their portfolios to their students. Presenting portfolios to students might help them see the rigors and complexity of teaching and learning, as well as the dedication and professionalism of their teachers. Presentations, such as these, also could help learners to view their teachers as fellow participants in the school's community of learners and scholars. For example, one portfolio producer not only presents her completed project to her students, but also involves them in her goal-setting and collection and selection activities. She sometimes asks students to decide which one of their works should be included in her professional portfolio and then asks them to explain, in writing, the reason for their selection.

Self-Reflecting about the Process and Product

The teacher who has completed a professional portfolio needs to examine whether the time and effort used to produce this tangible record were worthwhile. This examination can be an extension of the reflective aspect of the portfolio process, where once again, teachers can adopt and adapt strategies they have used to help their students achieve metacognition. Camp's (1992) questions about creating the final version of a student-writing portfolio can be changed to apply to teaching portfolios. For example, teachers can reflect upon how they think their teaching has changed over the year and whether this change was the result of producing a portfolio. Portfolio producers can examine and evaluate their efforts by considering whether they met their objectives and by ruminating about whether they feel or believe that their instruction has improved. Teachers need to think about the final portfolio product; they also need to analyze the process they used to achieve the product. Typically, producers of professional portfolios report that their initial questions about procedure and focus have been answered or refined by the end of the process. However, they often lament that these original "easy" questions have been replaced by "harder" questions about why they do what they do.

Teachers have come to realize that they need continually to revise their approach to the professional portfolio process based on their own personal experiences with the process. Portfolio producers need to decide if they value the product as a "horizontal" record of their progress, or if they want to expand and amplify this professional portfolio so that it becomes part of a "vertical" record of years of teaching. Most importantly, the supervisor has to decide whether or not he/she and the portfolio producer consider these final, personal ruminations of such significance that they must be included in the portfolio to provide closure for the portfolio process.

THE PROMISE OF PORTFOLIOS FOR NOVICE AND EXPERIENCED TEACHERS, PROFESSIONAL GROWTH, AND SCHOOL RENEWAL

What is the potential of portfolios for the improvement of teaching, learning, and schooling?

The Potential for Transformation

The process and production of a teacher/teaching professional portfolio can be as messy and as diverse as the process and production of a student portfolio. Nevertheless, both types of portfolios provide a systemic approach or frame that honors the fact that learning, for both student and teacher, is a process and a product. Portfolios are tangible evidence of growth and success. Additionally, as Yancey (1992) concluded that writing portfolios are paradoxically an assessment tool with the powerful potential to transform writing classrooms, so it can be concluded that teacher professional portfolios have similar paradoxical functions and power. The development and the final product of the professional portfolio can be used simply as an assessment tool by the producers, or it can be part of the formal assessment of the producers by their supervisors.

Significantly, the portfolio process and product have the potential to transform teacher/administrator relationships. Teachers and administrators can come to view their relationship as less adversarial and more collaborative as they work together to help teachers transact with, analyze, and improve their practice. Both parties can come to realize that the positional power of administration does not matter so much as does the professional purpose that they both and each feel as a result of collaborating in the production of a professional portfolio. Portfolios also have the power to transform what teachers think about themselves. Teachers are at the center of the collection, selection, and reflection processes. The choices that they make implant and reinforce personal autonomy, responsibility, independence, and self-management. Portfolio producers are challenged to take charge of their own performance and thereby to act as responsible professionals.

Although the production of a professional portfolio is an admirable accomplishment, it is not a goal that of and by itself will guarantee teacher renewal or improvement. The process and production of a portfolio is a tool that teachers can use to assess their strengths and needs. They can use this assessment, combined with other forms of evaluation such as formal or informal administrative observations, to develop goals for professional growth and improvement. The progress toward these goals can, in turn, direct portfolio collection, selection, and reflection.

For these reasons, it is essential that teachers examine their portfolio process and product to consider the concept of "systemic validity:" Will the goals they have selected promote the kinds of instructional changes that support learning for and by all students?

Farr and Trumbull (1997) identified criteria for valid alternative classroom assessments that can be equally and justifiably applied as ways for teachers to judge whether their portfolios are a valid teacher assessment alternative. For example, teacher as well as student portfolios should be linked to curriculum and content standards, promote higher-level thinking skills, and contain opportunities for self-assessment.

In addition to validity, it is important that teachers consider whether or not their portfolios demonstrate reliability: Do they measure or assess what they say they are measuring or assessing? In other words, are the artifacts selected, collected, and reflected upon true indicators of accomplishment of a portfolio goal, purpose, or objective? To consider the reliability of their portfolios, producers can utilize the ideas of efficacy and craftsmanship defined in the cognitive coaching paradigm (Costa & Garmston, 1994). Teachers can ask themselves if the evidence they have gathered has helped them to perceive that they are sharpening their ability to produce positive learning results. They can consider whether artifacts and their accompanying reflections have helped them reach their portfolio goals.

The Portfolio as a Form of Staff Development

For both the supervisor and the teachers, the compilation of a professional portfolio has the potential to be part of an efficient and effective staff development program. Like other good, relevant staff development activities, the portfolio production takes place within the context that is most important to teachers: Their own classroom and their own school. The process and product have the potential to effect and improve what goes on in the teachers' classrooms and schools. The ideas of relevance and practicality make the portfolio an appealing professional development activity for teachers who feel and know that their time is limited and precious.

Collecting, selecting, and reflecting about what one actually does and why one does it can be time intensive and energy consuming. But the benefits are numerous, readily apparent, and easily transferable to future situations. For example, if portfolio producers identify that they would like to investigate and try a new teaching strategy, the acts of investigation and implementation cause participants to examine what they are currently doing, to begin to change this behavior by using the new strategy, and then to compare and contrast the new strategy with previous practice. The use of the strategy provides teachers with immediate feedback. Moreover, such immediate feedback when placed in the context of the professional portfolio process and product has the power and potential to affect and improve future instruction as teachers become researchers who examine and analyze their actions.

Paradoxically, this process serves to both separate and integrate: It can enhance teachers' feelings of self-determination and autonomy, while providing opportunities to feel part of the school and teaching communities. The production of a professional portfolio is a collaborative and participatory process that involves dialoguing and interacting with one's supervisor and oftentimes with one's peers to refine procedural strategies and content. The participatory nature of this process can serve to alleviate and remediate the feelings of loneliness and isolation that many teachers report.

Additionally, like other effective staff development activities, the production of a professional portfolio has the power to meet a variety of purposes for different individuals. The portfolio is not a one-dimensional model with rigid requirements and outcomes that must be achieved by all. Instead, it can be used to meet and enhance institutional goals, instructional improvement, and personal goals, simultaneously and/or individually (Vacca, 1989). This means that a portfolio can be tailored to each individual's needs and expectations. Some participants might produce work that can be classified as defining and proving their competency in a particular area or technique of teaching. Other participants might produce work that demonstrates growth toward achieving a personal or institutional objective. Others might compile a portfolio that presents a picture and evaluation of their overall teaching performance. Still others might design a product that illuminates their career—who and what they are as teachers and professionals.

Just as the production of a professional portfolio has the power to meet a variety of purposes for different individuals, the process, like all effective staff development, can produce a variety of changes in those who participate and in the schools where they teach. All participants will not have the same experiences as they work through and toward the process and product. Their experiences will be based on a unique interaction of personal characteristics and of institutional and administrative expectations. All participants will not benefit equally from the process.

For example, one teacher who abandoned the portfolio project after one year's participation commented that he did so because he did not see that the time spent in collection, selection, and reflection was worth it. He felt that he had to "give up" or compromise other aspects of his life that were more important to him personally such as sports coaching. Another teacher complained that after three years of portfolio process and productions, rather than becoming a routine or integrated part of her professional goals and life, the portfolio had become a burden—"another thing to do." However, other participants report that they will keep "doing" their portfolios forever because they have become such an integral part of who they are as teachers and professionals.

Finally, such "vertical" production of multiple-year portfolios or the refinement of a single portfolio over a number of years again demonstrates that this process and product have potential for effective staff development. This "vertical" production can become part of a continuing process that unites producers, peers, and administration in a planned sequence of professional growth activities.

The Advantages of Portfolio Production for Both Teacher and Administrator

For the supervisor/administrator, the production of a portfolio by a teacher engages both parties in a collaboration that can be liberating. Liberation for the administrator can mean that the process and production of professional portfolios can facilitate change from a transactional leadership style that involves bartering with teachers to achieve better performance, to a transformative leadership style that unites administrator and teachers in a joint pursuit of formally agreed upon goals (Sergiovanni, 1990). Liberation and self-renewal for the administrator can also mean that the administrator feels that he/she is no longer alone and solely responsible for the verification of teachers' successes or failures. When the act of supervision becomes a people-oriented collaboration, liberation and self-renewal for the administrator can also result. The portfolio partner now bears more of the responsibility for his/her own teaching and the evaluation of his/her performance. The portfolio process and product are not limited to their uses as powerful personal, administrative, and/or institutional assessment tools. The process and product have other important uses such as serving as a communication medium between teaching peers and as a record of teacher experimentation and research.

Professional portfolios can be viewed by administrators as a facet of staff development that has the potential to help individual teachers be more self-reliant and responsible as they document, direct, and record their own professional growth by providing direct and first-person evidence of what is going on in a classroom. Portfolio process and product also can facilitate and frame teacher thinking, teacher/teacher interactions, and administrator/teacher relationships.

The Disadvantages of Portfolio Production for Both Teacher and Administrator

Although the development of professional portfolios has many positive aspects for the teacher and the administrator, no supervisor should believe that this process and product are without problems. Inappropriate or ill-defined portfolio procedures can cause participants to disagree about the effectiveness of the portfolio for teacher improvement and evaluation. For this reason, it is essential that the administrator, at least during the first year of a teacher's participation, presents the producer with some type of framework or expectations. These guidelines can be as simple as requiring the teacher to meet with the supervisor each month and requiring his/her product to contain a teaching philosophy and a table of contents. Such requirements focus both parties' responses, yet are not so supervisor-dominant as to restrict the teacher's activity, creativity, and growth. However, the listing of minimal expectations for either the process or the final product can be misinterpreted by the teacher.

It is also important that supervisors and producers work toward understanding that a portfolio is not merely a lesson plan book expanded and called by another name. Although like a lesson plan book, a portfolio can record classroom activities, the portfolio goes beyond recording to include reflections about teaching and learning.

Evaluation of the Portfolio Process and Product

In addition to establishing procedural guidelines as a way for a supervisor to avoid portfolio problems with a teacher, it is essential that both parties determine how the process and product will be evaluated. Will the method and product be discussed and agreed upon by both participants? Will the teachers have to prove that they have completed their portfolio objectives? What if they collect artifacts that document effort but do not indicate achievement of a goal? Will evaluation of success be determined by producer, supervisor, or both participants? Has the production of the portfolio really improved the teachers' teaching and students' learning? How can and will such improvement be documented?

It would seem that in the spirit of the collaborative dimension of the portfolio dynamic both parties would discuss the portfolio's evaluation. But how should a supervisor deal with a teacher who does not really collect, select, and reflect or seems incapable of doing this process? Sometimes the development of a professional portfolio can tell a supervisor positive things about a teacher that the supervisor did not know. On the other hand, portfolio production can tell a supervisor things about a teacher that the supervisor might not have known, might not have wanted to know, or does not know how to remediate. For example, how does one help a teacher who can not establish portfolio objectives? More importantly, what does this say about the teacher's ability to identify and delineate teaching unit and lesson objectives?

The production of a professional portfolio by teachers challenges the supervisors to work with producers to answer any and all of the questions raised about portfolio evaluation. It promotes a collaborative interaction that demands supervisors assume a new role. Supervisors do not function only as judges and evaluators; they serve as partners who help teachers extract meaning from their daily activities. This partnership is not without its risks for supervisors. They are asked to share responsibility and power with teachers, a practice which might not be comfortable for every administrator. Sharing responsibility and power implies that supervisors must come to terms with the same essential questions—who am I and why do I do what I do—that the portfolio process and product ask of teachers. It is also true that just as the portfolio process and product can become time-consuming for a teacher—"another thing to do"—it can also become a burden for supervisors. The opinion and criticism of other administrators may also pose a problem for supervisors. Critics might question why their fellow supervisor is trying the portfolio process. Don't they all have enough to do already? Is the supervisor trying outdo his/her peers?

While the professional portfolio has the potential to become part of a dynamic and recursive relationship between the producer, his/her portfolio, his/her teaching, his/her learning, and his/her supervisor, both parties—teacher and supervisor—need to understand that the development of a professional portfolio and the collaboration it entails are not easy. The change in perceptions and roles that are the result of this effort can be troublesome and threatening for those who participate and sometimes even for those who do not.

Administrative Modeling of Portfolio Production

One possible way for administrators to better comprehend the professional portfolio process and production is for them to model the procedure for teachers. This means that administrators will actually produce their own portfolios as examples of how to accomplish the task. Of course, during the course of this modeling, just as portfolio production enlightens teacher practice, supervisors who produce professional portfolios will learn about themselves and their success through the process. The development of a supervisor portfolio helps the administrator understand and empathize with the teachers and students. The production of a professional portfolio requires that supervisors exhibit behaviors and learning patterns that they expect from students and teachers.

Supervisors, like all portfolio producers, are required to make choices, experiment, and take risks. Supervisors must determine a clear purpose and objectives for their collection, selection, and reflection. This requires that they ask the same essential questions about themselves and their work that teachers and students ask when they compile portfolios. The development of a supervisor's portfolio has the same potential and power for self-renewal that is inherent in the process and product of teachers' professional portfolios.

Although there are similarities among student, teacher, and supervisor portfolio process and product, the development of a supervisor's portfolio offers some unique challenges. For example, the portfolio model implies a collaborative mode in which a participant shares his/her process and results. While supervisors could choose to collaborate with teachers as their partners, it is better to seek a partnership with another administrator who will provide the participant with the insight of a peer. It might be difficult for administrators to find peers who are interested in investing the time and effort needed to help another produce a portfolio.

One possible solution to this scarcity of willing partners is for the administrators who are interested in producing portfolios to seek each other out so they can serve as collaborators on each other's projects. Another possible solution is for administrators, either in the same district or same school, to collaborate on a single, joint portfolio that records artifacts relating to a district or school goal.

Because the purposes and objectives of supervisors' portfolios can be as varied as those of teachers, a most intriguing goal would be for a supervisor to produce a professional portfolio that has as its purpose, the documentation of teacher professional portfolio process and product. Teachers would be the natural collaborators in such an undertaking because they would be the subject of the research. Collection, selection, and reflection could involve both the teachers and the supervisor. Such interaction would reciprocally enhance each other's portfolio process and product.

The Connections between Current Educational Theories and Professional Portfolio Production

The production of professional portfolios has elements that are compatible with elements of current educational theories including constructivist learning theory, the cognitive coaching supervisory paradigm, and the school renewal concept of site-based planning and management. The process and production of a professional portfolio coincides with a constructivist view of learning if the teachers as portfolio producers are classified as the learners. Through collection, selection, and reflection, they are actively challenged to build a personal interpretation of their teaching and to learn how and when to improve their actions. Through the recursive process, the portfolio is produced in the real-world context of the classroom and the school. Practitioners then can use the knowledge they have gained about themselves and their teaching through portfolio production to alter and improve themselves and their teaching (Burke, 1994).

Constructivism has important ramifications for the supervisors and their role. The supervisor's role is not just that of an observer and evaluator. Supervision now focuses on working with teachers to construct knowledge about their own teaching and its effects on students' learning. The process and product of professional portfolios are also compatible with the cognitive coaching supervisory paradigm and the concept of Renaissance Schools outlined by Costa and Garmston (1994). All three concepts are undergirded by some similar beliefs: (a) Humans (including teachers!) make and construct meaning and knowledge from personal experience, (b) People can and do continue to develop intellectually, (c) Members of the school community are active and continuous learners, and (d) Leadership is the blending of the individual and the organization's needs and capabilities.

The development of professional portfolios requires that teachers, as individuals who are capable of actively and continually learning from their experiences, unite with organization goals to lead themselves and others. This definition of the process and product of professional portfolios is indeed compatible with the basic tenets of cognitive coaching and Renaissance schools. Thus, portfolios can be considered as an appropriate appendage to the cognitive coaching paradigm and the Renaissance schools concept.

The relationship between professional portfolio production and the school renewal movement of site-based planning and management is also compatible. Portfolio production and site-based planning and management require the stakeholders to examine and to take responsibility for what they are doing or for what they seek to change. Both are process oriented and request that participants identify goals and objectives and develop plans for achieving and documenting success. Furthermore, the production of professional portfolios can be incorporated into site-based planning and management by being listed as a tangible artifact that indicates completion of an action plan. In other words, the process and product of a professional portfolio can document completion of an objective, such as "to provide professional growth experiences that challenge teachers to analyze current practices."

While the production of professional portfolios can be seen as compatible to current learning theories and school renewal procedures, this process and product has the potential to create a community of learners, researchers, and scholars that extends beyond individual schools, districts, and states. The development of professional portfolios can be seen as part of a total process for institutional and personal evaluation, reform, and renewal that will result in institutional and personal nurturance and growth.

Through computer on-line communication and attendance at workshops, teachers and administrators have communicated with each other about their efforts, ideas, and ideals as they embark upon the relatively uncharted course of creating professional portfolios. Participants report that they have learned that portfolios are personally defined, yet collaboratively developed. Portfolios have been seen as more than a collection of teacher efforts; they also include student artifacts accompanying specific teacher lessons and/or goals and objectives. Portfolios also have been viewed as a manageable way to improve teaching and as a way to reflect who the teacher is as a professional. Portfolios are not just an array of teacher "stuff" or teacher craft.

Veteran teachers and administrators report that they can get excited again about what they are doing because they view portfolio production as a "positive" way for educators to interact. One educator states that she believes, "I must do this for me" as a form of self-reflection and actualization. She elevates the portfolio process and product further when she comments that many educators are working toward a better future for themselves and their students through the process of self-reflection that is such an integral part of professional portfolio development.

CONCLUSION: THE PROFESSIONAL PORTFOLIO AS A GROWTH PROCESS AND DISCOVERY TOOL

The production of professional portfolios is a growth process that involves true discovery and inquiry learning by both the administrator and teachers. The original project that precipitated this writing was the result of one supervisor and ten teachers questioning how could they strengthen their relationship with each other and improve student learning. They thought that the idea to produce a professional portfolio modeled on student portfolios was an original discovery. But like other discoveries, as they worked together during their first year, they came to find out through their readings and conversations that groups of teachers and administrators throughout the United States were also fledgling portfolio participants. During the past three years, the project has grown to include about fifteen teachers with the original supervisor. Other teachers in the building who have a different supervisor have also joined the ranks of portfolio producers.

This record of professional portfolio initiation and implementation is not meant to be a fool-proof guide or formula for professional growth, teacher development, or even portfolio production. Instead, it can be seen as a guide for reflection for other teachers who, after learning about the process and product, would be challenged to begin collection, selection, and reflection about their own teaching. It could also be used by teachers and administrators who are already participating in professional portfolio production as a comparison and contrast to their own efforts.

ACKNOWLEDGMENTS

The author would like to acknowledge her debt of gratitude to the portfolio producers at the West Windsor Plainsboro (NJ) Middle School who have challenged her to collect, select, and reflect upon her purpose and mission as an administrator.

The author would also like to thank her family for their belief in her and their patience with her efforts to record what she believes is a "noble experiment " that has the potential to transform teacher evaluation.

REFERENCES

Blase, J., & Kirby, P. (1992, December). The power of praise—a strategy for effective principals. *NASSP Bulletin*.

Burke, K. (1994). *The mindful school: How to assess authentic learning*. Palatine, IL: IRI/Skylight.

Camp, R. (1992). Portfolio reflections in middle and secondary classrooms. In K. B. Yancey (Ed.), *Portfolios in the writing classroom: An introduction*. (pp. 61–79). Urbana, IL: National Council of Teachers of English.

Costa, A. L., & Garmston, R.J. (1994). *Cognitive coaching: A foundation for Renaissance schools*. Norwood, MA: Christopher-Gordon.

Dietz, M. E. (1993). *Professional development portfolio/facilitator's guide*. San Ramon, CA: Frameworks.

Farr, B. P., & Trumbull, E. (1997). *Assessment alternatives for diverse classrooms*. Norwood, MA: Christopher-Gordon.

Ingalls, B. (1993). Interviewing a portfolio. In K. Gill (Ed.), *Process and portfolios in writing instruction* (pp. 63–68). Urbana,IL: National Council of Teachers of English.

Kouzes, J. M., & Posner, B. Z. (1987). *The leadership challenge.* San Francisco: Jossey-Bass.

Sergiovanni, T. (1990). *Value-added leadership: How to get extraordinary performance in schools.* New York: Harcourt, Brace, Jovanovich.

Vacca, J. L. (1989). Staff development. In S. B. Wepner, J. T. Feeley, & D. S. Strickland (Eds.), *The administration and supervision of reading programs* (pp. 147–162). New York : Teachers College Press.

Wolf, K. (1996) Developing an effective teaching portfolio. *Educational Leadership, 53* (6), 32–36.

Yancey, K. B. (1992). Portfolios in the writing classroom: A final reflection. In K. B. Yancey (Ed.), *Portfolios in the writing classroom: An introduction.* (pp. 102–116). Urbana, IL: National Council of Teachers of English.

Zubizarreta, J. (1994). Teaching portfolios and the beginning teacher. *Phi Delta Kappan,* 75(4), 323–326.

ABOUT THE AUTHOR

Alyce Hunter received her doctorate in Foundations of Education from Lehigh University. She is a supervisor of language arts, reading, and social studies curriculum and teaching for the West Windsor Plainsboro, New Jersey School District. She also teaches at the Graduate Schools of Education for both Wagner College and the College of New Jersey. Dr. Hunter is on the Board of Directors of the New Jersey Council of Teachers of English and the New Jersey Council for Social Studies. She has chaired the state level competition for the National Council for Teachers of English Literary Magazine Contest. Dr. Hunter has served on the National Council for the Social Studies Committee to Recognize Programs of Excellence and will be chairperson of this committee. Numerous articles and reviews written by Dr. Hunter have been published in journals such as *The English Journal, The English Leadership Quarterly,* and *Journal of Adolescent and Adult Literacy.* Dr. Hunter has been a presenter at state and national coventions on topics including teacher portfolios, interdisciplinary instruction, and middle school education. Dr. Hunter received a National Defense Department grant to plan and implement workshops and presentations to teach American teachers about China and Chinese culture. She received a Korea Society Fellowship to study and teach in Korea and a Fulbright Fellowship to study in Japan.

Subject Index

Author and Title Index